MAXWELL LAND GRANT

MAXWELL LAND GRANT

Facsimile of 1942 Edition
by
William A. Keleher

New Foreword
by
Marc Simmons

With a Preface
by
Michael L. Keleher

SANTA FE

New Material © 2008 by Sunstone Press. All Rights Reserved.

No part of this book may be reproduced in any form or by any electronic or mechanical means including information storage and retrieval systems without permission in writing from the publisher, except by a reviewer who may quote brief passages in a review.

Sunstone books may be purchased for educational, business, or sales promotional use. For information please write: Special Markets Department, Sunstone Press, P.O. Box 2321, Santa Fe, New Mexico 87504-2321.

Library of Congress Cataloging-in-Publication Data

Keleher, William Aloysius, 1886-1972.
  Maxwell land grant : facsimile of 1942 edition / by William A. Keleher ; new foreword by Marc Simmons ; with a preface by Michael L. Keleher.
    p. cm. -- (Southwest heritage series)
  Originally published: Santa Fe, N.M. : The Rydal Press, c1942.
  Includes bibliographical references and index.
  ISBN 978-0-86534-619-2 (softcover : alk. paper)
 1. Maxwell Land Grant (N.M. and Colo.)--History. 2. New Mexico--History--1848- I. Title.

F802.M38K4 2008
333.1'609789--dc22
                           2007051030

WWW.SUNSTONEPRESS.COM
SUNSTONE PRESS / POST OFFICE BOX 2321 / SANTA FE, NM 87504-2321 /USA
(505) 988-4418 / ORDERS ONLY (800) 243-5644 / FAX (505) 988-1025

The Southwest Heritage Series is dedicated to Jody Ellis and Marcia Muth Miller, the founders of Sunstone Press, whose original purpose and vision continues to inspire and motivate our publications.

CONTENTS

THE SOUTHWEST HERITAGE SERIES / I

FOREWORD TO THIS EDITION / II
by
Marc Simmons

PREFACE TO THIS EDITION / III
by
Michael L. Keleher

FACSIMILE OF 1942 EDITION / IV

I

THE SOUTHWEST HERITAGE SERIES

The history of the United States is written in hundreds of regional histories and literary works. Those letters, essays, memoirs, biographies and even collections of fiction are often first-hand accounts by people who wanted to memorialize an event, a person or simply record for posterity the concerns and issues of the times. Many of these accounts have been lost, destroyed or overlooked. Some are in private or public collections but deemed to be in too fragile condition to permit handling by contemporary readers and researchers.

However, now with the application of twenty-first century technology, nineteenth and twentieth century material can be reprinted and made accessible to the general public. These early writings are the DNA of our history and culture and are essential to understanding the present in terms of the past.

The Southwest Heritage Series is a form of literary preservation. Heritage by definition implies legacy and these early works are our legacy from those who have gone before us. To properly present and preserve that legacy, no changes in style or contents have been made. The material reprinted stands on its own as it first appeared. The point of view is that of the author and the era in which he or she lived. We would not expect photographs of people from the past to be re-imaged with modern clothes, hair styles and backgrounds. We should not, therefore, expect their ideas and personal philosophies to reflect our modern concepts.

Remember, reading their words and sharing their thoughts is a passport back into understanding how the past was shaped and how it influenced today's world.

Our hope is that new access to these older books will provide readers with a challenging and exciting experience.

II

FOREWORD TO THIS EDITION
by
Marc Simmons

It has been my privilege over many years to meet quite a few of the Southwest's leading historians. I first began seeking them out when I was in elementary school and took the measure of each one, to see what I could learn from them about the history craft.

On November 19, 1966, I visited William A. Keleher at his home not far from downtown Albuquerque, New Mexico. We sat in his living room for an hour or so, talking about New Mexico's golden past and he inscribed a couple of his books I'd brought along. After more than 40 years, the specifics of our conversation that day have dimmed. But I do recall coming away with the firm impression that I had been fortunate to spend a bit of time with a master historian.

In fact, Will Keleher spent most of his adult life as a practicing attorney and a civic leader. Yet on the side, he managed to publish four major books about 19th century New Mexico, plus a volume of his memoirs that began in 1892 and extended to the end of the 1960s. In my own *Albuquerque, A Narrative History* (1983), I relied heavily on Keleher's recollections to capture the spirit and flavor of life in the city that he had known intimately at the turn of the century.

Born in Lawrence, Kansas, William was only two years old when his family moved to Albuquerque in 1888. That was just eight years after arrival of the railroad and the founding of New Albuquerque at trackside. Thus, the boy and the town grew up together.

In 1900 at age 14, Will was hired as a Western Union messenger to deliver telegrams by bicycle throughout the business district. On his own, he began studying Morse Code and soon was able to send and receive telegrams.

"At that time," Keleher would declare later, "Albuquerque was a genuine Wild West town." Gambling was wide open and the municipal government paid its expenses by collecting fines from madams in the red light district. Hangings, legal and otherwise, were not uncommon, while fires and floods regularly troubled the community. Will Keleher saw it all growing up, and it left him with a sense of being a part of history.

William A. Keleher as a young man.
Photograph courtesy of Michael L. Keleher.

In 1907 he took a job as a reporter on the *Journal* and a few years later became city editor for the old *Albuquerque Herald*. The experience gained as a journalist would stand him in good stead when down the road he began writing history. Before that, however, he acted upon what he called "a long cherished wish to attend law school." The school was Washington & Lee in Virginia. Returning to Albuquerque with his degree in 1915, he practiced law there for much of the remainder of his life.

So what was it that turned Attorney William Keleher toward a parallel career as a New Mexico historian? Clearly, several things contributed to that end. One was his association with many frontier figures, beginning with an aging former Santa Fe Trail trader Franz Huning, to whom he had delivered telegrams as a boy, and through his long friendship with famed gunfighter Elfego Baca.

Other factors mentioned by Keleher himself were his newspaper reporting and his legal training. Owing to those things, he said, "it was only natural that the time would come when I would have the urge to write."

His first book, *Maxwell Land Grant* (1942), was published by Santa Fe's then prestigious Rydal Press. In it, Keleher led the way in sorting out the long and confusing history of that enormous grant in northeast New Mexico. His research led him to the conclusion that each one of the old Spanish and Mexican land grants had a human interest story connected with it.

Maxwell Land Grant was followed by *The Fabulous Frontier* in 1945 (revised in 1962), containing robust sketches of men like Thomas B. Catron, Sheriff Pat Garrett, rancher John Chisum, and Senator Albert B. Fall. Each left a strong imprint on New Mexico's history in the years before statehood.

Book three in Keleher's quartet of histories was *Turmoil in New Mexico, 1846-1868* (1952). In vivid and precise detail, he carved out explosive stories of the American conquest of New Mexico, the Confederate invasion during the Civil War, and the saga of the last great Navajo war that led to the tribe's exile on the Pecos river.

And finally, Keleher brought out his *Violence in Lincoln County* (1957), adding much new information on the troublous times there in the long period from 1869 to 1881.

To the dedication and self-discipline necessary for such large production must be added the reminder that William Keleher, in the midst of his scholarly labors, carried on his very active law career. He even found time to serve a term as president of the New Mexico State University board of regents.

Honored as one of the state's foremost historians, William A. Keleher died on December 18, 1972.

Sunstone Press by bringing Keleher's books back into print in its highly acclaimed Southwest Heritage Series gives a new generation of readers access to these valuable works of regional history. The author's legacy deserves to be preserved.

III

PREFACE TO THIS EDITION
by
Michael L. Keleher

William A. Keleher observed first hand the changing circumstances of people and places of New Mexico until his death December 18, 1972, surrounded by family. He was born in Lawrence, Kansas November 7, 1886, and arrived in Albuquerque two years later, with his parents and two older brothers. The older brothers died of diphtheria within a few weeks of their arrival. One quickly observes from his writings, and writings about him, he lived a fruitful and exemplary life. He was recognized as a successful attorney, being honored by the New Mexico State Bar as one of the outstanding Attorneys of the Twentieth Century. His knowledge and understanding of humankind is evidenced by his quote attributed to Sir Thomas Browne, 1686, and printed after the title page in *Turmoil in New Mexico*:

> The iniquity of oblivion scattereth her poppy and deals with the memory of men without distinction to merit and perpetuity...who knows whether the best of men be known, or whether there be not more remarkable men forgot, than any that stand remembered in the known account of time.

An insight to his character and religious belief is indicated by the last paragraph of the Foreword to his *Memoirs*, First Edition:

> The writing of this book has afforded me an opportunity for study and reflection while attempting to recall what was said or done by people in the long ago, many of whose voices are stilled forever. During this time, I have experienced a renewed consciousness of the significance and vital importance of recognition of God's eternal verity.

His dedication and love of family and New Mexico is shown by the concluding paragraph of *Memoirs* by which he bequeaths his "respect for the law and my love for New Mexico" to his children, grandchildren and nephew.

William A. Keleher in later life.
Photograph courtesy of Michael A. Keleher.

His great joy seemed to be to have someone call at his house or stop him on the street and ask him to autograph one of his books, which he did gracefully, with a twinkle in his eye and some individual remembrance or personal comment after a short visit with the admirer. On more than one occasion he remarked the changing circumstances of people and places he knew would be forgotten forever. It became his single-minded purpose to record his observations of persons and circumstances so they would not be forgotten, and avoid the "iniquity of oblivion".

Anyone who reads his books will enjoy an increased awareness of people and places of New Mexico, and they too will become an heir to his respect for the law and love for New Mexico.

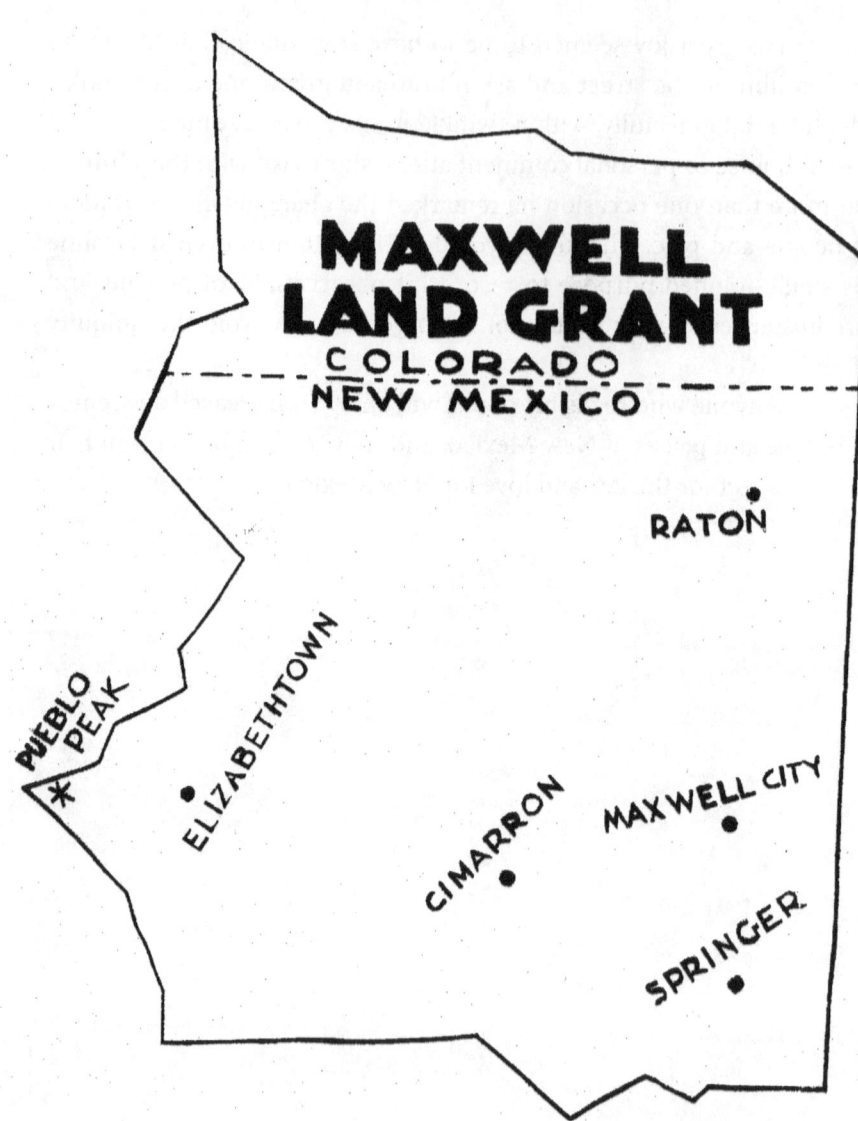

IV

FACSIMILE OF 1942 EDITION

MAXWELL LAND GRANT

Lucien B. Maxwell

MAXWELL LAND GRANT

A New Mexico Item

By William A. Keleher

The Rydal Press, Santa Fe, N. M.

Copyright 1942
By WILLIAM A. KELEHER

oCDo

Manufactured in the
United States of America
by
THE RYDAL PRESS
Santa Fe, New Mexico

oCDo

Cover Design and
Case Binding by
HAZEL DREIS

Dedicated to
the Memory of
My Father and Mother
DAVID KELEHER
MARY ANN GORRY KELEHER

Foreword

No attempt has been made here to do more than to give an outline of the history of the Maxwell Land Grant in New Mexico and southern Colorado, and to briefly sketch the characters dominating an enterprise that would have challenged the ambition and the best efforts of almost any man or group of men in America of the Seventies and Eighties. The Grant contained a vast area of land, almost 2,680 square miles; its history spans an entire century of time. Under different circumstances the Grant might have become for New Mexico a second Salt Lake, Utah, area. It has not been considered possible or desirable to attempt to cover all of the ramifications of the Grant history. Neither has it been deemed appropriate to tell of the many fine enterprises conceived and executed in the modern days of the Grant ownership. A separate volume would be required to tell the story of the projects undertaken on the Grant and carried foward successfully to develop the gold, silver and coal properties; to tell of the construction of irrigation works and railways; to tell of the development of the lumber industry; to tell of the immense and important cattle and sheep ranches on the Grant; to tell of the many successful agricultural enterprises. All of these things, along with the story of the magnificent estates established by wealthy people, are in the field of a writer who has the inclination to carry forward the story of the Grant from the time the last evicted squatter picked up his belongings and moved on, under court order, to some place else, God knows where, just so it was not on the Maxwell Land Grant. It has been possible to make only passing reference to the establishment in 1891 of the New Mexico Court of Private Land Claims, by Act of Congress, a court composed of high-minded and intelligent men, who in a few short years accomplished much in straightening out the tangles of New Mexico land grant titles. The Court deserves a volume in itself.

In presenting the work I wish to record here grateful thanks and appreciation to Hon. George Curry, of Kingston, New Mexico, now in his eighties, with mind and memory strong and clear; to Mrs. Adeline J. Welborn, of Fort Sumner, and Mrs. Michel Nalda, of Vaughn, New Mexico, granddaughters of Lucien B. Maxwell, for their personal recollections; to Mr. Marion L. Fox, of Albuquerque, for kindly assistance and encouragement; to Mr. Fred W. Kirkpatrick, of Albuquerque, who kindly made available to me the bound volumes of the Las Vegas Gazette for the years 1872 to 1882; to Monsignor Jules N. Stoffel, of Albuquerque, for the use of fugitive documents on land grants in New Mexico; to Hon. E. C. Crampton, of Raton, for kind permission to study valuable documents and transcripts in his ownership; to Miss Ilda B. Sganzini, for assistance in research and indexing; to Mrs. Ellis Dean Neel, for secretarial work; and to my sister, Julia M. Keleher, of the University of New Mexico, for assistance in revision. I must assume full responsibility for any statement of fact, for dates, citations and like information. My principal hope has been to furnish a regional contribution that may possibly help to indicate to the young men and women of New Mexico the significance of the Seventies and Eighties in one part of their native state.

WILLIAM A. KELEHER

Albuquerque, N. M., November 15, 1942.

Contents

	Foreword	ix
I	Briefly About Land Grants	3
II	Miranda and Beaubien	13
III	Rights on the Grant	21
IV	Lucien B. Maxwell	25
V	Maxwell, the Real Estate Man	39
VI	The Indians	45
VII	The Cimarron Country	67
VIII	Ministers of the Gospel	75
IX	Anti-Grant Litigation	83
X	The Vigilantes	99
XI	The Supreme Court	109
XII	The Financial Aspects	113
XIII	Spanish Americans	119
XIV	Claims of Land Stealing	125
XV	Judge Vincent and Grover Cleveland	135
XVI	Dawson's Ranch and A. A. Jones	141
XVII	"Steve" Elkins and "Tom" Catron	149
	Sources	155
	Index	157

Illustrations

LUCIEN B. MAXWELL	Frontispiece
MAXWELL GRIST MILL AT CIMARRON	6
DELUVINA MAXWELL	24
PETER MAXWELL AND HENRY J. LEIS	40
LUZ BEAUBIEN MAXWELL	72
KIT CARSON HOME AT RAYADO	72
LUCIEN B. MAXWELL HOME AT FORT SUMNER	88
GEORGE CURRY	120
PETER MAXWELL GRAVE	136

MAXWELL LAND GRANT

CHAPTER I
Briefly About Land Grants

A GLANCE at an officially prepared map of New Mexico will disclose that much of the territory embraced within its boundaries in the north and central part is identified as land that was a gift or a grant from either Spain or Mexico. The granting of land in New Mexico, whether under Spanish or Mexican rule, was for centuries a most significant and important factor in the colonization of New Mexico. Many an acre of New Mexico land traces its ancestry back to royalty.

In the year 1511, Ferdinand II of Spain established a governing board, which was remodelled by Charles V in 1524, providing for the exclusive management of the affairs of the Spanish colonies in the Americas. This board is known in history as the Supreme Council of the Indies. Theoretically, the King of Spain presided over the Council and all important acts were subject to his sanction and confirmation. The Spanish colonies in America were divided into four vice royalties, of whch Mexico was one, and New Mexico was a part of Mexico. The three others were Peru, Rio de la Plata (Buenos Aires) and New Granada. There were, in addition to the vice royalties, five captain generalships, for the government of Yucatan, Guatemala, Chile, Venezuela aand Cuba. The captains general were independent of the viceroys and the viceroys were independent of each other.

The Royal Audience was established in the City of Mexico in 1528, with the viceroy installed as ex officio president. The Audience was composed entirely of Europeans and possessed vast power over all civil and ecclesiastical tribunals. The viceroy in Mexico City was not given specific power to grant lands, but on the theory that he was in effect the King of Spain, he apparently assumed that he possessed that power.

New Mexico continued under the jurisdiction of the Audience of Mexico City for two centuries, from 1528 to 1728. Under Spanish law, promulgated June 16, 1617, colonial officers could grant lands, but title did not pass definitely until the grant had been confirmed by the King of Spain. During the period extending from 1524 to 1827, covering more than three centuries, a great many laws and regulations were in effect, under Spanish rule, having to do with land granting in the colonies, and most of these applied to grants of land in New Mexico. The great distance on land and sea between New Mexico and Spain, the length of time required in connection with correspondence, and the decline in the power of the King of Spain in connection with confirmation of grants, all tended toward uncertainty and difficulty in connection with land titles. As a result, it is certain that a land grant problem existed in New Mexico, as well as in other parts of the Spanish colonies, during the years of Spanish rule; and it is equally certain that a like land grant problem existed in New Mexico during Mexican rule. Consequently, when the United States of America acquired New Mexico by invasion and conquest on August 15, 1846, it inherited a land grant problem of considerable magnitude.

During the many years of its rule, the Kingdom of Spain had a specific interest in New Mexico and its welfare. There was a policy, definitely expressed in Law 66, Title 2, Book 3, Recopilacion de los Indias, that "New Mexico be fostered, and that Viceroys of New Spain appoint the governor there." A brief part of the law bearing the marginal endorsement of Philip the Third, at San Lorenzo, on Nov. 1, 1609, was as follows:

"We charge and command the viceroys of New Spain

to aid and favor the conversion and pacification of New Mexico, so that for the lack of evangelical laborers and other necessities preaching shall not fail to spread abroad through these provinces as far as possible . . . . . observing and causing to be observed what is ordered in regard to newly discovered regions, and they confer the government of those provinces on persons of much intelligence."

With reference to land distribution Book IV, Title XII, Law X of the Recopilacion provided that, "Lands shall be distributed with excess among discoverers, and old settlers, and their descendants, who are to remain in the country and those best qualified shall be preferred. . . ."

Iturbide took the City of Mexico on Sept. 27, 1821, establishing the independence of Mexico. On January 3, 1823, the national council of Mexico passed a colonization law, providing for two kinds of grants of land, one to promoters, called empresarios, to be made by a contract executed between the empresario and the government of Mexico, and the other to individuals, to be made by the common councils, called ayuntamientos. New Mexico was made a territory of Mexico under Mexican law on July 6, 1824, and was made a Department of Mexico on Dec. 3, 1836.

From time to time Mexico amended, abrogated and repealed laws, rules and regulations pertaining to land grants. Consequently its land grant policy was not consistent between the years 1821 and 1846, the quarter of a century that elapsed between the time of its revolt against Spanish rule and the conquest of New Mexico by the United States. Both under Spanish rule and Mexican rule the granting of lands was not a simple transaction. Many pitfalls stood between the grant and the final confirmation, and there was always the possibility of a revocation of the grant for legal or political reasons. Doubtless political influence, close friendship and other factors entered into the granting and holding of lands. Long service in the army was one of the principal supporting reasons advanced in petitions for grants. With vast areas of land to be granted, the officials could afford to be generous in making the donations of land, especially if it appeared that there was any possibility of colonization or of building up a frontier against the ever present menace of the Indians.*

A treaty of "Peace, Friendship, Limits and Settlements," between the United States of America and the Mexican government was dated at Guadalupe-Hidalgo, on February 2, 1848, ratified and confirmed as required by the laws of both nations, and formally proclaimed by the President of the United States on July 4, 1848. Under article eight of the treaty, citizens of Mexico, then residing in territory previously belonging to Mexico, had the option for a period of one year to arrange their affairs, and to decide whether they wished to continue citizens of Mexico or become citizens of the United States, all of their property rights to remain secure regardless of their decision. At the time of the signing of the treaty, and its proclamation by the President of the United States, large tracts of land in New Mexico were owned by citizens of Mexico in the form of land grants. The grants had been made for the most part in what are now known as Colfax, Mora, San Miguel, Rio Arriba, Sandoval, Santa Fe, Bernalillo and Socorro Counties, roughly the northern and central part of New Mexico. Strange to say, few, if any grants, were made on what may be called the eastern tier of counties in New Mexico. The early colonists required water for domestic and irrigation purposes and favored grants of land along the Rio Grande and its tributaries, which

---

* For detailed references to the history and laws relating to grants, see "Spanish and Mexican Land Laws," by Matthew G. Reynolds, Santa Fe, N. M., Aug. 15, 1895; Hall's "Mexican Law," 1881. For a brief resume, see "Law of the New Mexico Land Grant," by W. A. Keleher, Texas Law Quarterly, Oct. 1929, pp. 154-169.

Maxwell Grist Mill at Cimarron

accounts largely for the grants in a number of the counties in the northern and central part of New Mexico. Hostile Indians, coupled with lack of an abundance of running water, probably account for the absence of grants in the eastern part of New Mexico, perhaps a fortunate circumstance in view of the oil development of recent years in the counties of Lea and Eddy.

Having inherited a land grant problem by the conquest of 1846 and the treaty of 1848, nothing was done by America to solve the difficulties in connection with it, until July 22, 1854, when the Congress of the United States enacted a law creating a Surveyor General for New Mexico, with the obligation to follow the instructions of the Secretary of the Interior, "to ascertain the origin, nature, character, and extent of all claims of lands under the laws, usages, and customs of Spain and Mexico." (See U.S. Stats. at Large Vol. X, p. 309.) The Surveyor General was obliged to make a full report on all claims of land grants, with his decision as to the validity or invalidity of the titles. The report of the Surveyor General, under the law of 1854, was to be made to the Secretary of the Interior, who in turn was to submit the report to the Congress of the United States, with a view to confirming bona fide grants, thus giving full effect to the Treaty of 1848. The law of 1854 proved a cumbersome method of solving the problems incident to titles to land grants. The Surveyor General was given a task entirely beyond the ability of any one man. Surveyor General after Surveyor General struggled with the flood of land grant claims that were filed in his office. Claims were approved or disapproved and reports were submitted to the Secretary of the Interior, who in turn submitted reports to the Congress. The Congress of the United States was not equipped with the machinery required to cope with the land grant problem. Some claims were confirmed off hand, after a hurried study by members of a committee. Other claims languished indefinitely, receiving no attention. The claims approved by Congress were generally those with the most persistent advocate on the outside, and the most powerful political influence on the inside.

Every governor of New Mexico without exception from 1856 to 1889, complained about the condition of the land grant titles in New Mexico in annual reports, in special messages to Congress and otherwise, but it was not until March 3, 1891, that the President of the United States approved a land court bill, entitled, "An Act to Establish a Court of Private Land Claims." Enactment of the bill followed an emphatic recommendation to the Congress for such legislation in the President's message on December 1, 1889, and a special message on July 1, 1890. The court was organized at Denver, Colo., July 1, 1891, and achieved every objective sought by the backers of the legislation.

The land grant titles of New Mexico for decades had been locked up in pigeon holes either in the office of the Surveyor General in Santa Fe, in the office of the Secretary of the Interior in Washington, or in the desk of some committee member of Congress in the Capitol building, naturally more interested in obtaining the appointment of a postmaster in his home state than in unraveling the intricacies of a New Mexico land grant. During the wait of forty years and more, death had come to many grant claimants, and their descendants had frequently sold their rights for a fraction of their true value. The condition of the grant lands and their claimants was deplorable.

In his annual report to the Secretary of the Interior for 1881, Governor Lionel A. Sheldon remarked, when dealing with the land grant problem: "Charges of fraud and crime are made as to some grants that have been confirmed, such as forgery of papers, perjury, subornation of perjury, and false and erroneous surveys. This fact and the lapse of time challenge the utmost scrutiny into the grant claims that may be presented in the future."

BRIEFLY, ABOUT LAND GRANTS

In his report to the Secretary of the Interior for 1883, Governor Sheldon said:

> "New Mexico is largely plastered with grants of land, real or pretended, made by the Spanish and Mexican governments. By law these grants are segregated from the public domain, and must continue in a condition of practical mortmain until final action is taken to determine their validity. The claimants do nothing to develop or improve or pay taxes on them, and a satisfactory title cannot be acquired by others. In some cases the grants overlap, which leads to disputes and occasional acts of violence. Confirmations have been carelessly made and it is generally believed that errors and frauds have been practiced and apparently legalized through want of knowledge of or attention to the subject. Grants have been confirmed of greater dimensions than the Spanish or Mexican laws seem to justify, and though mineral lands were not alienated in fee simple by those governments, still confirmatory acts have been passed and patents issued, under which it is claimed that minerals pass to patentees. Success in securing confirmation of grants of a doubtful character so encouraged and emboldened the covetous that it is alleged the manufacture of grant papers became an occupation, and surveys have been so erroneously made as to lead to a belief that these grants are endowed with India rubber qualities."

Edmund G. Ross, governor of New Mexico in 1885, resurrected politically from his long exile, after having served in the United States Senate from Kansas during the impeachment trial of President Andrew Johnson, wrote scathing messages on the land grant situation during his term as chief executive of the Territory.

"It is now nearly forty years since New Mexico became a territory of the United States," wrote Gov. Ross in his message of 1885 to the Secretary of the Interior. "In 1854 an effort was made to institute a system of adjudication whereby titles in land grants could be perfected. But instead of accomplishing that purpose, these titles have become from year to year more complicated, till they are now in a far worse condition than at the time of the annexation."

Governor Ross had a word to say about methods pursued to enlarge grant boundaries:

"So common has this practice become of enlarging the boundaries of bona fide grants made by Spain and Mexico, and so general and apparently well grounded is the suspicion that there has been in operation for many years a systematic and cunningly executed scheme for the manufacture of fraudulent titles to large tracts of public domain under the guise of Spanish and Mexican grants, that the public faith in all such titles has largely diminished. That fact has, in turn, not unnaturally, but none the less unjustly, weakened faith in titles to lands in this Territory to such a degree as to discourage investment and consequent development."

L. Bradford Prince, one of the best educated, and perhaps the most prolific writer on New Mexico affairs to serve as governor of New Mexico in Territorial days, complained repeatedly about land grant titles.* In his annual report to the Secretary of the Interior dated Oct. 12, 1889, Governor Prince patiently restated the case for New Mexico on land grant titles, saying:

"So much has already been said on this subject by

---

* Both Lew. Wallace, of Indiana, and Edmund G. Ross, of Kansas, who had preceded Prince as Governor of New Mexico, were prolific writers, but did not write particularly on New Mexico or New Mexico subjects.

BRIEFLY, ABOUT LAND GRANTS

others that there is little to be added. I will simply recapitulate the leading points in the fewest words by reminding you that New Mexico differs entirely from the remainder of the territories in this respect; that it is an old and not a new country; that it was settled years before Jamestown, New Amsterdam or Plymouth; that for over two hundred years it was under Spanish control, and for a quarter of a century was a part of Mexico; that during that long period it was under a system of law, relative to land titles, entirely different from ours; that when acquired by the United States, all the land that was owned at all was held under the laws or customs of Spain or Mexico, and that, considering its vast extent and considerable population, those holdings were naturally very numerous. A change of sovereignty, of course, did not affect private rights; and it will be doubted whether the best course as to land titles would not have been to have left them to be determined in the courts, as if no sovereignty had taken place."

During the period from 1854 to 1870 the Congress of the United States, either on recommendations of the Surveyor General of New Mexico, of the Secretary of the Interior or on its own initiative, confirmed sixty-two Spanish or Mexican land grants. Suddenly in 1870, the Congress changed its policy and declined to act at all on any New Mexico land grant claim. Among the grants that had been confirmed by Congress was the Miranda and Beaubien, or Maxwell Land Grant, and the story of that grant is taken as the dominant theme of this work.*

* Both under the Spanish and Mexican law, small parcels of land could be granted to individuals. The granting of small tracts, in theory, was not greatly different from the homestead laws of the United States of America. Poor recording facilities, lost documents and inability to prove that a grant had been made worked great hardship on many small land holders following the American Occupation. The Grants by Mexico had been specifically provided for under the regulations of Nov. 21, 1828, under the Mexican colonization act of August 18, 1824. The government of the United States finally made provision for proving up of these claims, known as Small Holding Claims, with justice to the claimants.

CHAPTER II
Miranda and Beaubien

THERE was submitted to Governor Manuel Armijo in Santa Fe on January 8, 1841, a petition for a grant of land, drafted in the language and style of the day, signed by Guadalupe Miranda, a citizen of Mexico. It was also signed by Carlos Beaubien, born in Canada, but who had become a Mexican citizen and who was a resident of San Fernandez de Taos. The petition was unusual in that it was an exposition of conditions as they then existed in New Mexico. In the first few lines, it was set forth, "that of all departments in the republic, with the exception of the Californias, New Mexico is one of the most backward in intelligence, industry and manufactories." "Surely," the petition read, "few others present the natural advantages to be found therein, not only on account of its abundance of water, forests, wood, and useful timber, but also on account of the fertility of the soil, containing within its bosom rich and precious metals, which, up to this time, are useless for the want of enterprising men who will convert them to the advantage of other men, all of which productions of nature are susceptible of being used for the benefit of society in the Department of New Mexico as well as in the entire republic, if they are in the hands of individuals who would work and improve them."

The lands of New Mexico, the petitioners said, would be useless to the department unless reduced to possession and worked. "The department," the petition continued, "abounds in idle people, who for the want of occupation, are a burden to the industrious portion of society . . . idleness, the mother of vice, is the cause of crimes which are being daily committed . . . the towns are overrun with thieves and murderers. . . . We think that it will be a difficult task to reform the present generation, accustomed to idleness and hardened in vice. But the rising one, receiving new impressions, will easily be guided by the principles of a purer morality. The welfare of the nation consists in the possession of lands which produce all the necessaries of life without requiring those of other nations; and it cannot be denied that New Mexico possesses this great advantage, and only requires industrious hands to make it a happy residence."

Peering into the future and expressing some hope for salvation of New Mexico, the petitioners struck a hopeful note: "This is the age of progress and the march of the intellect, and they are so rapid that we may expect at a day not far distant, that they will reach even us."

Present day farmers might be interested to know that Miranda and Beaubien had definitely in mind a specific plan for cultivation of crops on the lands for which they were asking. The petition mentioned, among other things, the raising of sugar beets. "Under the above conviction," the petition concluded, "we both request your excellency to be pleased to grant us a tract of land for the purpose of improving it, without injury to any third party, and raising sugar beets, which we believe will grow well and produce an abundant crop, and in time to establish manufactories of cotton and wool, and raising stock of every description."

The description of the land desired to be granted, burdened with the ambiguities that were to create so much trouble and litigation in later years, was contained in the final paragraph of the petition. On January 11, 1841, three days after the petition had been presented, the following brief message was penned by Governor Armijo:

"Santa Fe, January 11, 1841.
"In view of the request of the petitioners, and what

they state therein being apparent, this government, in conformity with law, has seen proper to grant and donate to the individuals subscribed the land therein expressed, in order that they may make the proper use of it which the law allows.

ARMIJO."

Apparently Miranda and Beaubien did nothing of importance to reduce the land to possession and ownership for some two years after Armijo's act, for on February 12, 1843, at Taos, they petitioned Don Cornelio Vigil, Justice of the Peace, to consider them as having presented themselves requesting execution without delay of their rights in connection with the Grant. On February 13, 1843, Justice of the Peace Vigil signed an order promising possession, and on February 22 of the same year, executed a document reciting that he had proceeded to the land described in the petition, had erected mounds to mark the boundaries, which corresponded with the plat submitted to him, and to which he attached his rubric. The plan of Miranda and Beaubien to take over and occupy the land met with active resistance on the part of Rev. Antonio Jose Martinez, Curate of Taos, who had always opposed large grants of land to wealthy persons, claiming that the lands should be granted to poor people. Father Martinez vigorously contended in papers filed in Santa Fe and elsewhere that a part of the land granted to Miranda and Beaubien conflicted with lands claimed by Charles Bent, and that a large portion of the land involved belonged to the people of Taos, and other towns, that such lands had been long known as commons and the people had for generations grazed their livestock on them. Martinez claimed among other things that the land had been granted to foreigners, apparently referring to Beaubien and Charles Bent.*

---

* Charles Bent was appointed Governor of New Mexico Sept. 22, 1846. He was assassinated in Taos, January 19, 1847. Charles Bent and Padre Martinez were bitter enemies.

In a letter written by Charles Bent to M. Alvord, in Santa Fe, dated Taos, January 30, 1841, Bent was very sarcastic in his references to Padre Martinez. To quote one part of the letter, which among other things demonstrates that Bent was not very proficient at spelling:

> "You ask me for local nuse of this place, I shall endeavor to give you such as has come to my hearing. The greate literry Martianes since his return has been the all interesting topic. He has been cept constantly imployed since he got home detailling to his gready admirers and hearers, the greate respect and attention that was bestowed on him in his last trip to Durango, he says that he is considered by all whoe he had the opportunity of conversing with, as one of the greatest men of the age, as a literary, an eclesiastic, a jurist, and a philanthoripist and moreover as he has resided in one of the most remote sections of this province intirely dependent on his own resorses for such an immense knoledge as he has acquired, it is astonishing to think how a man could posibly make himself so eminent in almost every branch of knollidge that can only be acquired by other men of ordinary capasitys in the most enlightened parts of the world, but as he has extraordinary abillities, he has been able to make himself master of all this knollidge by studing nature in her nudest gise, he is a prodigy, and his greate name deserves to be written in letters of gold in all high places that this gaping and ignorant multitude might fall down and worship it, that he has and dare condisend to remain amongst and instruct such a people, it is certainly a great blessing to have such a man amongst us, theas people cannot help but find favor in this and the other world in consiquence of having such a man to leade and direct them; if the days of

miricals had not gon by I should expect that God would bestow some greate blessing on theas people through this greate man, and possibly whenever the wise rulers of this land heare of the greate fame of this man they will no doubt doe something for theas people in consideration for the greate care of this more than Solomon."

The plea of Padre Martinez for a stay of the Grant was successful to the extent that the rights of Miranda and Beaubien were suspended, through an appeal by Martinez to the supreme government of Mexico for an investigation into the Grant that had been made by Governor Armijo. The order of suspension was signed on February 27, 1844, by Don Mariano Chavez, who was at the time interim governor of New Mexico. On April 13, 1844, Manuel Armijo had been re-appointed to the office of civil and military governor of the department, and two days later, April 15, 1844, the departmental assembly gave its opinion sustaining the Miranda and Beaubien claim to the Grant.

Beaubien in his efforts to persuade the authorities that the settlers in the Taos area had no objection to the Grant, had presented a pleading setting forth his grievances because of the delay that had been caused by the action of "the Curate of Taos," including a declaration signed by Pablo Lucero and some ten others. The Lucero statement was designed to overcome the claims of Padre Martinez that the lands were common grazing lands and for years had been a buffalo hunting ground. The benefits to come from the efforts of Miranda and Beaubien were pointed out:

> "There is no objection made to the proposed settlement," the Beaubien statement argued, "it being well known that the lands have never been used as pasture grounds for cattle, and not for a long time as a buffalo

hunting ground. The settlement of the grant would be a benefit to the interior settlements, affording them protection from the enemy in that direction, occupying a great number of idlers who have no occupation in the cultivation of the soil, and relieving this vicinity from a large number of persons who crowd us. The endless difficulties we experience every year on account of the scarcity of water for irrigation would be avoided. But the greatest advantage to the entire department would be, that in case of a war with the Navajo Indians, the stock could be pastured during the entire year in the vicinity of these new settlements, and be protected by them. It is also certain that from Taos to the Arkansas River there are not more than six or seven days journey traveling with packs at a moderate pace; from here to Rayado one and one-half days journey; from the head of the Red River to the Arkansas, from three to four days."

The American Occupation found Miranda and Beaubien in technical possession of the lands which they claimed under the Grant of 1841 from Governor Armijo. On September 15, 1857, through their counsel, Houghton, Wheaton and Smith, Guadalupe Miranda and Charles Beaubien presented their claim to William Pelham, Surveyor-General of the Territory of New Mexico. They set forth their contention that the lands they described in their petition had been granted to them by the Governor of New Mexico, under the Mexican Republic, confirmed and approved by the departmental assembly of New Mexico, and claimed that they had cultivated and improved portions of the land for the preceding twelve years. The tract, the petition set forth, had never been surveyed, and the claimants were therefore unable to furnish any certain estimate of its contents; that a small portion only was fit for cultivation, and the balance, owing to its mountainous character and scarcity of water, was useless for any other purpose than that of pasturage.

On July 28, 1857, Christopher Carson, noted Indian fighter, was a witness before Surveyor-General William Pelham, of New Mexico, in regard to ownership of the Grant. Carson testified that he had passed there as early as 1844 with Lucien B. Maxwell and at that time had seen large fields of growing corn, beans and pumpkins; that he had known the place well since 1845, at which time he observed that several houses had been built on the big Cimarron and another house on one of the smaller streams on the Grant. In 1845, Carson testified, he and Richard Owens and others had gone on the Grant, and settled there. He had built a house for himself and cultivated fifteen acres in garden and feed, but had been obliged to leave hurriedly for California in August of that year without harvesting his crops. Lucien B. Maxwell, according to Carson's testimony, had settled on the Rayado, a stream within the Grant, in 1849, and "is there now." In response to a question as to the extent of the improvements on the Grant, Carson testified there were 200 acres of land under cultivation, buildings of a value of about $15,000 and that 15,000 head of livestock grazed on the Maxwell ranch.

On September 25, 1857, Surveyor-General Pelham rendered a decision, holding that the Grant was good and valid according to the laws and customs of the government of the Republic of Mexico and the decisions of the Supreme Court of the United States, as well as the Treaty of Guadalupe Hidalgo of February 2, 1848. The Grant was confirmed in Guadalupe Miranda and Charles Beaubien and the papers were transmitted for final action to the Congress of the United States. On June 21, 1860, the Congress, by an act entitled, "An Act to Confirm Certain Private Land Claims in the Territory of New Mexico," 12 St. at L. 71, confirmed the Grant with a description identical with the one contained in the petition submitted to Governor Manuel Armijo, which was as follows:

> "The tract of land we petition for to be divided equally between us commences below the junction of the Rayado River with the Colorado, and in a direct line toward the east to the first hills, and from there running parallel with said River Colorado in a northerly direction to opposite the point of the Una de Gato, following the same river along the same hills to continue to the east of said Una de Gato River to the summit of the table land, from whence, turning northwest to follow along said summit until it reaches the top of the mountain which divides the waters of the rivers running towards the east from those running toward the west, and from thence following the line of said mountain in a southwardly direction until it intersects the first hills south of the Rayado River, and following the summit of said hills toward the east to the place of beginning."

For many years the description was most important in the labors of surveyors, lawyers, judges, land speculators, government officials, and assumed much significance in the lives of many of the common people.

CHAPTER III

Rights on the Grant

FROM Governor Manuel Armijo, to Miranda and Beaubien, and from them to Lucien B. Maxwell, down almost to the present day, the Maxwell Land Grant has had no counterpart in the story of land grants in New Mexico. The Indians, early Mexican and Spanish-American settlers, early American pioneers, the latter seeking homesteads and settling on what they believed to be free land, each in turn, discovered in the end, that they had no rights which were superior to "grant rights". Geographically, since January 25, 1869, when the legislature of New Mexico created Colfax County, the Maxwell Land Grant in New Mexico has been situated within that county. The 265,000 acres located within the State of Colorado, were originally within New Mexico, but thrown into Colorado when the line between New Mexico and Colorado was straightened out by Act of Congress in 1861.

Before bits of land had been taken away to make up other counties, the County of Colfax embraced a vast area, bounded on the north by the State of Colorado, on the west by Taos County, the original home of the Maxwell Land Grant, on the east by Texas and Indian Territory, the present day Oklahoma, and on the south by Mora County. The central and western parts of Colfax County, as originally organized, were traversed by the Red River, Chicorico, Una de Gato, Vermejo, Ponil, Cimarron, and Rayado, never failing streams of immense importance to agriculture and to the livestock industry. The southern and eastern portions of the County were traversed by the

Rito Plain, Sweetwater, Ocate and the Coyote in the Black Lake Country.*

Because of an abundance of water and wide valleys of great fertility, high mountains, great forests and plentiful grass, wild animals in great numbers had their habitat in many parts of the Maxwell Land Grant, and it was especially attractive to buffalo, antelope, grouse, bear and deer. The rivers and streams in early days were alive with fish. The Plains Indians, in the days before the mountain men, and for many years after, certain of finding deer, beaver and fish in the country, made it one of their principal places for fishing and hunting. For generations the Indians of the Plains had met with the Apaches, Navajos and Pueblo Indians, and even with the Indians from the far off Gulf of Mexico, for trading purposes at places near Cimarron.

There was an established custom that at certain times of the year Indian wars and attacks would cease to permit peaceful trading between and among the tribes. The Indians considered the country described in the Miranda and Beaubien Grant as their own territory. They had traveled over it from time immemorial; they had fished in its waters and streams; they had hunted over its mountains and plains. Even as late as the seventies and eighties, the Ute and Jicarilla Indians believed that they were the real owners of the country embraced within the Maxwell Grant. Many years were to pass before they could be brought to understand the white man's talk that there had been a Grant, that a governor of New Mexico under Mexican rule had given the land away to a French-Canadian named Beaubien and a Mexican citizen named Miranda, and that through strange and devious ways, control of the land had gotten finally into the hands of American, British and Dutch capitalists.

Drifting out from Taos and other villages, settlers of Spanish and Mexican descent had for generations established homes and ranches on the Cimarron, on the Rayado and other streams, and

*See Rep. of Sec. of Interior 1895-1896, p. 498.

in pleasant valleys, grazing their sheep and cattle on the hills and mountains, cultivating the land, believing in the best of faith that they were the real owners of substantial parts of the Grant. Many years passed before they too, finally realized that a vaguely known Supreme Court of the United States, had ruled that they really had no ownership in the land upon which they and their ancestors had lived for many years, the soil of which they had cultivated, the grazing lands of which they had used, fenced and occupied for a life time.

The American settler, the Gringo, had less complaint than the Indian or the settlers of Spanish and Mexican ancestry. Many of the American settlers were comparatively latecomers. They took up land on the Grant, and improved it on the strength of announcements from the Department of the Interior from time to time that later on the Grant would be surveyed, that it would be divided into townships and sections. The Gringos for many years were under the impression that squatters' rights would in due time ripen into homesteaders' rights, and that the government of the United States would validate and respect those rights.

Land-hungry Americans, lately discharged, in the late seventies and early eighties, from service in the army at nearby Fort Union, settled on the Grant in the Moreno Valley. Other Americans came from Iowa, Illinois, Kansas, and other states by wagon train, in prairie schooners, and were settled by land agents. The Americans, for the most part, could not help but know that there was grant trouble and that eventually they might not receive a good title to the land on which they were settling. Some Americans, especially ex-soldiers from Fort Union who settled in the Moreno Valley, never acknowledged any superior title, nor relinquished their rights. As to them, their occupation finally became adverse, ripened into perfect title, more so by reason of the presence of a shotgun or Winchester rifle behind the kitchen door than by any paper evidence of title. In due time, however, most of the American settlers found out, as the Utes and Jicarilla Indians before them had found out, and as settlers of Spanish and Mexican ancestry had discovered, that obtaining title to a tract of land on the Maxwell Land Grant by squatting, by hopeful homesteading, was a task too difficult for the average man. There was always assurance of certain litigation, expense, endless turmoil and attendant fears.

Small wonder that the man looking for a homestead turned his eyes toward Colorado, Utah, California, returned to Texas or to the state from which he had come; or hitched up his team of horses or mules and "vamosed".

Many Indians, Americans, Spanish-Americans, however, refused to give up their rights without a fight. Colfax County for years was divided into two camps, "grant" men and the "anti-grant" men. The "grant" men for the most part were employed by owners of the Grant, or profited through the existence of one of the companies organized to take over the activities in connection with the project. "Anti-grant" men were all the small homesteaders and ranchers, men who were settling in the country, and who could receive no assurance that they were on or off the Grant, and people generally who had small sympathy with "land grabbing". The anti-grant faction claimed that the boundaries of the Maxwell Land Grant had been stretched into fantastic dimensions. In the seventies and eighties the charge was freely made that promoters of the project "moved mountains" and "changed the names of rivers" to extend the boundaries of the Grant. Naturally the women, wives of claimants and homesteaders, were vitally interested in the grant fight, and sometimes became more aggressive than the men.

Deluvina Maxwell, Friend of "Billy the Kid"

CHAPTER IV
Lucien B. Maxwell

LUCIEN B. MAXWELL, New Mexico pioneer, with a career as colorful as any of the early western trail blazers, arrived in Taos in 1841, intending to make that place his residence. On June 3, 1844, at Taos, Maxwell married Luz Beaubien, daughter of Charles Hipolite Trotier de Beaubien, a Canadian, and Paulita Jaquez Lavat, part French, part Spanish. It would be interesting to trace the ancestries of Lucien B. Maxwell and of Luz Beaubien and to refer to the achievements of members of their families on both sides, but that field is left to the genealogist. Born in Kaskaskia, Illinos, September 14, 1818, Lucien B. Maxwell was the son of Hugh Charles H. Maxwell, a native of Dublin, Ireland, who came to America in 1799, and of Marie Odile Menard Maxwell, of the Menard family, distinguished in the early history of Illinois.

After a life of great adventure and remarkable achievements, Lucien B. Maxwell died at Fort Sumner, New Mexico, on July 25, 1875. Charles Beaubien, father-in-law of Maxwell, had been a resident of New Mexico since 1823. In his youth Beaubien had studied for a time for the Roman Catholic priesthood, but realizing that he had no call to the religious life, drifted west, settled in Taos and married in 1827. In Taos, with its Spanish environment, the name Charles Beaubien soon became the euphonious Carlos Beaubien.

Beaubien was for many years very prominent in public affairs in New Mexico. When Brig. Gen. S. W. Kearney soon after the American Occupation searched for three judges of the newly formed New Mexico Civil Court, who would be loyal to the United States of America, he appointed Carlos Beaubien one of them on September 22, 1846. Judge Beaubien, a remarkable character in many ways, died in Taos on February 10, 1864. His wife, born December 28, 1811, died on August 13, 1864, and was buried near the old Maxwell home place in Cimarron. Luz Beaubien Maxwell, Judge Beaubien's daughter, died on July 13, 1900, twenty-five years almost to the day, after the death of her husband, Lucien B. Maxwell.

Well-educated, considering the period during which he lived, Lucien B. Maxwell was described as being five feet ten and one-half inches in height. He was stockily built, of fair complexion, with blue eyes and brown curly hair. Unfortunately Lucien B. Maxwell kept no diary, was not a careful bookkeeper, wrote few letters, enjoyed a joke, but was not fond of talking about his early adventures or discussing his business affairs. The story of Lucien B. Maxwell's life must be pieced together from the odds and ends still available.

Sixty-seven years after his death, the grave of Lucien B. Maxwell is not identified by any marker or monument, not too comforting a thought to his descendants or to those who appreciate the value of his contribution to the history of his adopted New Mexico. In politics Lucien B. Maxwell was a member of the democratic party, although there is only one known instance of activity in party affairs. He attended a meeting called to reorganize the democratic party in Santa Fe, on December 15, 1874.

Luz Beaubien, who became the wife of Lucien B. Maxwell in 1844, was a beautiful woman, with large hazel eyes, dark hair, and complexion like "milk and roses" according to Deluvina Maxwell, her long time personal servant.

When Lucien B. Maxwell married a daughter of Carlos Beaubien, he married into the affairs of the Miranda-Beaubien Grant. Don Carlos Beaubien probably owned a full half interest in the

Grant, although Charles Bent had acquired an interest, possibly from both Beaubien and Miranda, at a time and for a consideration unknown. Narcisse Beaubien, a son of Charles Beaubien and Paulita Jaquez Lavat Beaubien, who was to have looked after the land interests of the family, was killed by Indians in the Revolution at Taos in January, 1847. The management of Beaubien's interest in the Grant logically fell to Lucien B. Maxwell. Maxwell acquired outstanding interests in the Grant from time to time and eventually became the owner of the entire property, by that time known as the Maxwell Land Grant, but not without difficulty and much litigation.

When he settled down in Taos in the Forties and married, Lucien B. Maxwell, although still a very young man, gave up a life of great adventure. He had been with the Fremont expedition in the exploration of the Rocky Mountain regions and with Fremont expeditions in California.*

Later Maxwell was a trapper on the Columbia, Platte and Arkansas Rivers. He was a companion and associate of St. Vrain, Charles Bent, Kit Carson, Richard Owen and others of that band of pioneers who penetrated into a part of Mexico prior to its acquisition by the United States, and all of whom were remarkable for their ability and force of character.

Lucien B. Maxwell was with John Charles Fremont on at least two of his expeditions, the first and second. The first Fremont expedition occupied the summer of 1842 and scouted the country between the Missouri River and the Rocky Mountains, along the line of the Kansas and the Great Platte or Nebraska River. The expedition was assembled at St. Louis and it was there, according to Upham's "Life Explorations and Public Services of John Charles Fremont, Boston, 1856," that "Mr. L.

---

* Lucien B. Maxwell had been engaged on May 22, 1843, by Fremont, as a hunter, and Christopher (Kit) Carson, as the guide, in St. Louis, on the exploration of the country lying between the Missouri River and the Rocky Mountains on the line of the Kansas and Platte Rivers. See "Report of J. C. Fremont to Col. J. J. Abert, March 1, 1843," in "Travels in the Great Western Prairies, Thomas J. Farnham, 1843."

Maxwell was engaged as a hunter and Christopher Carson, celebrated the world over for his genius and exploits as a mountaineer, and everywhere known as Kit Carson, was the guide of the expedition." Fremont started on his second expedition in the spring of 1843. Lucien B. Maxwell traveled from Taos and joined the party in Kansas. Kit Carson joined the second expedition on July 14, 1843, at the point, "where the Boiling Spring River enters the Arkansas," according to Upham. On Fremont's Fourth Expedition, which began on October 19, 1848, Fremont was in Taos where he had a reunion with Kit Carson and Lucien B. Maxwell. Fremont reported that "Maxwell is at his father in law's doing a very prosperous business as a merchant and contractor for the troops." That Fremont had small regard for "Bill Williams," of Rocky Mountain fame was made known in a letter written by Fremont to his wife from Taos on January 27, 1849. Fremont, in Upham's Life, tells the story:

> "At the Pueblo, I had engaged as a guide an old trapper well known as 'Bill Williams', and who had spent some twenty-five years of his life in trapping in various parts of the Rocky Mountains. The error of our journey was committed in engaging this man. He proved never to have in the least known or entirely to have forgotten, the whole region of country through which we were to pass. We occupied more than half a month in making a journey of a few days, blundering a tortuous way through deep snow which had already begun to choke up the passes, for which we were obliged to waste time in searching."

Fremont lost all of his mules and a number of men through dependence on "Bill Williams," but finally reached Taos, with members of the party more dead than alive.

Lucien B. Maxwell had only become fairly well settled in Taos when New Mexico was invaded and conquered by the

United States. As early as 1847, Maxwell began at Rayado, on the Grant, the erection of some buildings, and commenced building the town of Cimarron in 1857 and 1858. Rayado was a military post from 1847 to 1850. It is doubtful if Maxwell had the faintest conception, when he first settled on the Grant, of its potential acreage, being under the impression probably for many years that it contained between 32,000 acres and 97,424 acres, or twenty-two Spanish leagues. Nevertheless, people of Maxwell's time lived to see the day when the Grant was legally declared to embrace a total of 1,714,764.93 acres of land. The Grant held within its boundaries chains of mountains, rivers, creeks, wide valleys, thousands upon thousands of acres of fine grazing land, important mineral deposits, great areas of standing timber.

Anti-grant leaders claimed that the boundaries of the Maxwell Land Grant had been vastly extended through distorting the meaning of the words of the description, through political manipulation before administrative officers in both Santa Fe and Washington. The surveys of the Grant were made by surveyors employed in private practice, under a government contract, and not by surveyors whose salaries were paid by the government. There was little question but that the government of the United States paid scant attention to the surveys at the time they were being made. It was charged that the owners of the Grant assisted in the surveys by pointing out their contentions in regard to natural boundaries and offering advice in regard to what had been intended to be conveyed in the original grant description.

During the early years of Maxwell's ownership of the Grant, there was no outward manifestation of a claim to exclusive possession of any vast tract of land. Up to about 1868, Maxwell's Ranch, as it was called, on the Cimarron River, contained nothing under fence but the Maxwell residence, with adjoining corrals and stables, the conspicuous three-story stone structure of the grist mill, which has fought against the ravages of time and still stands, its walls intact, and some two hundred acres of farming land.

The grist mill was a landmark for the Indians, and from many miles away they traveled to Cimarron to watch its machinery grind grain into flour. Remnants of the Ute and Apache Tribes of Indians had their headquarters near the Maxwell Ranch, and drew their government rations at Cimarron. The Indians suffered as the result of indifferent, frequently changed policies of the federal government. They had always looked upon Lucien B. Maxwell as their friend and counselor. He had talked to the Indians, pacified them, urged patience in the face of stupidity of Indian agents, of shifting policies of the Commissioners of Indian Affairs in Washington. The Utes and Apaches, in return, at times protected the Maxwell Ranch and Maxwell's family from raids and depredations by other tribes.

The Indians hunted and fished on the Grant, entirely ignorant that any gift of what they considered Indian land had been generously made on January 11, 1841, by Governor Armijo of New Mexico, on behalf of Mexico, to Guadalupe Miranda and Carlos Beaubien, doubtless equally ignorant of the fact that Lucien B. Maxwell claimed ownership to their happy hunting grounds.

Pastoral and agricultural interests dominated the affairs at the Maxwell Ranch for twenty years, from 1848 to 1868. Lucien B. Maxwell was master of a great area of land, happily surrounded by his wife and six children, Peter Menard, Virginia, Emilia, Sofia, Paulita and Odile. Three other children had died in infancy. He had great pride in Peter Menard, only son of the family, and hoped that he would eventually succeed him in the management of his livestock and agricultural affairs. Peter Menard Maxwell, born April 27, 1848, and who died on June 21, 1898, was destined by fate to play an important part in the drama that was to be enacted at Fort Sumner, New Mexico, on July 14, 1881, when he witnessed the shooting of William H. Bonney ("Billy the Kid"), by Patrick F. Garrett.

Lucien B. Maxwell spoke Spanish beautifully, and although he never joined them, was sympathetic toward the Penitentes. In the springtime, on Good Friday of Holy Week, Lucien B. Maxwell understood that most of his men on the ranch would be in attendance at the morada doing penance. They were grateful to him, when on Easter Saturday, with the knowledge of wounds and lacerations suffered in atonement and penance, Lucien B. Maxwell would send food to break their fast, ointment and bandages to cure the hurts of their bodies.

When spring merged into summer, nothing pleased Lucien B. Maxwell more than to walk barefooted on his lands and dip his feet in the cooling waters of an acequia in the alfalfa fields, and discuss with his Penitente friends topics relating to field and farm, lambing, branding of calves, horse racing, the prevailing price of wool.

Suddenly during the idyllic days at Cimarron, the calm of Lucien B. Maxwell's life was broken, not by the whoop of warring Indians, but by the discovery of the secret and unexpected marriage of his daughter, Senorita Virginia Maxwell, to Captain A. S. B. Keyes, of the United States Army, who had been appointed Indian Agent at Cimarron to succeed Maxwell. The marriage took place on March 30, 1870, in the third story of the fortress-like stone grist mill belonging to the Maxwells, built in 1864, the interior of which had been decorated for the occasion with tanned skins of buffalo, bear, deer, mountain lion and other animals. The ceremony was performed by Rev. Thomas Harwood, Methodist missionary, with Mr. and Mrs. Isaiah Rinehardt as the only witnesses. Many years later Tom Harwood confessed that the Keyes-Maxwell marriage was the first and last that he performed, "contrary to the wishes of the parents."*

Virginia Maxwell, educated at a convent in St. Louis, was a

---

* History of New Mexico, Spanish and English Missions of the Methodist Episcopal Church, Vol. 1, Rev. Thomas Harwood, El Abogado Press, Albuquerque, 1908.

beautiful and charming young woman. She personally made all arrangements for the wedding. Rev. Thomas Harwood, advised by Miss Maxwell of her parents' opposition to her marriage to Captain Keyes, and of their desire that she marry a wealthy Spanish-American on the Rio Grande, finally consented to perform the ceremony. "She had it all planned," said Rev. Mr. Harwood. "No army general could have planned for a battle more wisely than she planned for this marriage. Virginia Maxwell had made a confidante of Mrs. Rinehardt, a good Methodist and the miller's wife. It was Indian ration day. There were hundreds of Apaches at the mill, drawing their rations of meat and flour."*

The marriage was kept a secret for several weeks after the ceremony, until Captain Keyes received expected orders to proceed to an Eastern post. When Lucien B. Maxwell learned of the secret marriage of his daughter, Virginia, to Captain Keyes, after their departure for the East, he became infuriated and went on the warpath.

Friends and foes of the Rev. Mr. Harwood sent him word that it would be well for him not to show up in Cimarron, Elizabethtown or the surrounding country. In one letter he was told that he was threatened with a ducking, in others with blacksnaking. With Cimarron and Lucien B. Maxwell on one side and hostile Apaches on the other, in his missionary country, Thomas Harwood was sorely beset. He finally had the matter out with himself:

> "I said to myself, I have been a soldier under Grant, Sherman, and Howard, and Logan, and Rusk, shall I now cringe like a cur before such fellows as these who are scraping and bowing to a rich man with the hope that they will, by so doing, get a few crumbs from his rich, two million dollar sale of his grant? I said, No,

---

* Ibid.

the Lord helping me, I will go up to Elizabethtown and fill my next Sunday appointment."*

When the missionary reached Elizabethtown, he learned that Lucien B. Maxwell had threatened to challenge him to a duel. Rev. Mr. Harwood finally made his way into Cimarron, and although he never met the Maxwells face to face, he later learned that they had finally become somewhat reconciled to the marriage. When the Maxwell Land Grant was sold, tradition has it that Maxwell went to New York City, met his daughter, gave her ten thousand dollars, and that they never met again. But the Maxwell-Keyes marriage caused Tom Harwood many sleepless nights. For many years Rev. Mr. Harwood was obliged to deny the story, widely circulated, that he had received a thousand dollars for marrying Virginia Maxwell to Captain Keyes. The minister said the marriage offering was only twenty-five dollars, and declared there was as much truth in the story as there was in another story floating about in the Cimarron country to the effect that Lucien B. Maxwell had been employed as a cook in Fremont's party in the Rocky Mountains, and had been discovered by Captain Fremont in the act of kneading with his bare feet the bread being prepared for the officers' table; and that Fremont had at once set him adrift in the mountains, without guide or compass to direct his way to any settlement in that unknown region.†

* Ibid.
† Rev. Thomas Harwood lived to see the success and happiness of the marriage of Capt. A. B. Keyes to Virginia Maxwell. Lieut. Maxwell Keyes their son, became an aide de camp to Col. Theodore Roosevelt in Cuba, was killed in action by the insurgents in the Philippines after the Spanish-American War. Their son, Col. Edward S. Keyes, of Fort Sam Houston, was for a number of years on the faculty of the New Mexico Military Institute, after having seen distinguished service in the Spanish-American War. A daughter, Lucy Keyes, married Col. Harold Fiske, of the United States Army. Captain, later Colonel Keyes who was born in Boston, and fought through the Civil War as a private, became a Colonel in the regular army after his Cimarron days. Both Col. Keyes and Virginia Maxwell Keyes are buried in the Presidio, San Francisco, Cal. Mrs. Keyes died in 1909. The marriages of the other Maxwell children were as follows: Peter Menard to Sadie Lutz; Sofia to Telesfor Jaramillo; Emilia to Manuel Abreu; Paulita to Jose Jaramillo; Odile to Manuel Abreu. Manuel Abreu married Odile after the death of Emilia.

It was not until 1867 and 1868, when it became generally known that gold had been discovered in the Moreno Valley, that the outside world began to pay any particular attention to the Maxwell Land Grant. When the gold rush started, men flocked to the Moreno Valley, to Ute Creek and Willow Creek on the Grant from all parts of the United States. They feverishly prospected for pay dirt in the mountains, canyons and valleys of the Maxwell Empire. For the first time, Maxwell felt obliged to assert ownership of the property and to demand royalty on all claims taken up on the Grant. Some men recognized Maxwell's authority, others hotly disputed it. Thus was born the fight over the title to the Grant.

Discovery of gold on the Grant was no great surprise to Lucien B. Maxwell. He had known for years that there was gold on the property. From time to time Indians, trappers and traders had brought gold nuggets to the Cimarron trading post and exchanged them for supplies. Maxwell put the gold in a chamois bag and occasionally amused his children by emptying the bag of nuggets on the floor for them to play with. Prospector friends of Maxwell had told him many times that there was rich gold-bearing ore on the Grant in the vicinity of what later became the famous Aztec mine.* Maxwell was indifferent to the placer gold nuggets with which his children played, and to the samples of ore left with him by the prospectors. He manifested little interest in the mining possibilities of his property, but was eventually forced to recognize them by the rush of goldseekers over-

* The Aztec mine, Baldy, New Mexico, on the Maxwell Land Grant, became a noted property. Placer gold was found on Willow Creek, on the west slope of Baldy Peak in October 1866. In 1867 placer mining began in this region, which later became known as the Elizabethtown district. About $2,250,000 in gold was found in the placers. The placer gold was found along streams heading on Baldy Peak, and in June 1868, the lode was discovered and the Aztec mine opened up, with a 15 stamp mill being put into operation on October 29, 1868. For a few years the yield was as high as $21,000 a week. A report in 1870 showed the ore was averaging $68.83 a ton saved on the plates. During the first four years of operation about $1,000,000 in gold was taken out of the Aztec mine. See U. S. G. S. Annual Report, George M. Wheeler, Appendix J. J. for 1876, containing examination of Alfred R. Conkling; and U. S. G. S. Bulletin 620 N. "The Aztec Gold mine, Baldy, New Mexico, by Willis T. Lee, 1916.

running the Grant, when the magic words, "Gold on Maxwell's Grant" finally were whispered from one to another.

Playing with the Maxwell children at Cimarron and toying with the gold nuggets, was Deluvina Maxwell, a Navajo Indian who had been captured by Spanish-Americans in the Canyon de Chelly country, when a child of nine, together with her sister, Maria, fifteen. On their way to hunt piñons, Deluvina's father, mother and three brothers had been killed by enemy Indians. Deluvina was captured and brought to the Cimarron country as a slave. Tradition has it that Maxwell purchased her freedom for ten dollars. Deluvina took the name of Maxwell and was ever after a member of the Maxwell family. She died in Albuquerque on November 27, 1927. When the Maxwells left the Grant and went to Fort Sumner, Deluvina went with them. She displayed her lack of fear the night of July 14, 1881, when she cussed out Pat Garrett, and entered the room where "Billy the Kid" lay dead. Garrett had shot and killed her friend, William H. Bonney, and Garrett, John W. Poe and other supposedly fearless men were reluctant to enter the room for fear that "Billy" might still be alive, and only waiting a chance to send them into Kingdom Come.

Big business of the day began to look into the possibilities of the Maxwell Land Grant when it was rumored that gold had been discovered on the Grant. Preliminary investigation of promoters demonstrated that there were possibilities of great coal, lumber and mineral production, above and beyond the grazing and farming possibilities. An inventory was taken of possible total acreage of the property, of its assets and potentialities. Almost before Lucien B. Maxwell was aware of what had happened to him, he was no longer master of the immense Grant, with its vast extent of land, its many streams, high mountains and wide valleys. Receiving $650,000 for his share of the sale of the property, Maxwell started life anew as he had done so many times in his youth, little expecting that he was making his last important move. With money at his command, Maxwell was induced to furnish the capital for the First National Bank of Santa Fe, but he knew nothing of finance, cared little for banking. His mind was on land and livestock, on the matching of pinto ponies against sorrels in a country horse race for a wager. Maxwell soon tired of the idea of banking, and in 1871 he sold his control of the bank in Santa Fe to Stephen Benton Elkins and Thomas Benton Catron.*

Having sold his vast land grant, Maxwell took over the old Fort Sumner property, then in San Miguel County, which had been abandoned by the government, following the failure of the attempt to compel the Navajo Indians to live there. Maxwell purchased the improvements which commanded thousands of acres of public grazing land in the Pecos River country, and with his old caporal, Jesus Silva, started to the new ranch. Although it had been an old buffalo hunting country, the new location was not greatly to Maxwell's liking. The Fort Sumner country was not to be compared with the Cimarron country. At Cimarron there had been blue grass and long stemmed gramma; water in great abundance and a vast extent of excellent summer and winter range, a kingdom that would have challenged the ambition of any man who believed he was destined to be an empire builder.

At Fort Sumner there were the old government buildings, the officers' houses, the parade grounds, plenty of public domain for grazing. There was the Pecos River, it is true, but, so different from his beloved Cimarron. Maxwell, on his new ranch, ran nine thousand head of cattle, some of them driven from the old Maxwell Ranches in the Cimarron and Rayado country, others purchased in the Fort Sumner country. He planted wheat, corn

---

* The First National Bank of Santa Fe was organized September 3, 1870. Lucien B. Maxwell furnished $150,000, the amount of paid in capital, took 1270 shares for himself, gave Charles F. Holly of Cimarron 200 shares, John S. Watts of Santa Fe, 10 shares, his son, Peter Maxwell 10 shares, and Henry M. Hooper of Cimarron, 10 shares. Lucien B. Maxwell was elected the first president of the bank, John S. Watts, vice-president, and Charles F. Holly, cashier.

and other grains at the new ranch, but his heart was not in the new venture. He made some poorly advised investments in railroad bonds; he lost substantial sums of money here and there. He was not happy.

The Utes and Jicarilla Apaches searched out his new home. They traveled down the Pecos on their ponies, and traded again with Lucien B. Maxwell, exchanging dressed buffalo hides for things they needed. But the distance from Cimarron to Fort Sumner was great. Riding to Maxwell's new home on a pony was a hardship. The visits of the Indians became less frequent, and finally ceased altogether. On April 15, 1875, Lucien B. Maxwell went from Fort Sumner to Rayado, where he sold to Matt Lynch, of Trinidad, Colorado, the big ditch, forty miles long, which conveyed water through the mountains to the mines at Elizabethtown. On May 22, 1875, Maxwell sent twelve men across the Staked Plains to Fort Sill, Indian Territory, to bring back horses that had been stolen from his Fort Sumner Ranch by the Comanche Indians. The men returned on July 3, 1875, trailing forty head of horses.

Never recovering from his longing for the Cimarron country, Lucien B. Maxwell was taken suddenly ill, became bedfast and died at Fort Sumner on July 25, 1875. A fast riding courier on horseback was sent for a doctor to Las Vegas, 150 miles away, and Dr. J. H. Shout started for Fort Sumner. A relay of saddle horses had been provided by the courier so that Dr. Shout could change mounts every twenty miles. Dr. Shout began the long ride on Monday morning, but upon reaching Elkins' ranch on the Pecos, eighty miles from Las Vegas, the physician learned of Maxwell's death, so he turned about and returned to his home.

Lucien B. Maxwell was buried in the cemetery at Fort Sumner, where officers and enlisted men who had died in the service of the United States had been buried. His estate, administered in San Miguel County, New Mexico, by his son Peter Maxwell, disclosed that although Lucien B. Maxwell had spent the bulk of his fortune, he was fairly well to do at the time of his death.

Those who laid Lucien B. Maxwell in his grave could not foresee that within a few years there would be placed in the same cemetery the body of William H. Bonney ("Billy the Kid"), and other outlaws, or that nine out of ten persons visiting the cemetery in the years to come would ask to see the place where the Kid was buried, and on learning that Lucien B. Maxwell had been buried in the same cemetery, ask with mild interest, "Who was Lucien B. Maxwell?"

An appraisal of the life and works of Lucien B. Maxwell was contained in an editorial in the Las Vegas Gazette of July 26, 1875, in the words:

> "Against Lucien B. Maxwell, no man can say aught, and he died after an active and eventful life, probably without an enemy in the world. Of few words, unassuming and unpretentious, his deeds were the best exponent of the man. He was hospitable, generous and upright, and dispensed large wealth, acquired by industry and genius, with an open hand to the stranger and the needy."

At the time of his death, July 25, 1875, it was said of Lucien B. Maxwell that no man in want, Indian, Mexican, Spanish or American, had ever crossed his threshold without being the recipient of his bounty.

CHAPTER V
Maxwell, The Real Estate Man

NOTED as a frontiersman, trapper and pioneer resident of New Mexico, Lucien B. Maxwell was also somewhat of a business man. He demonstrated ability to acquire real estate and sell for a handsome profit, to make money on government contracts. When land was turned into cash, Maxwell's judgment was not good. Certainly he was the most important individual real estate operator of his day in New Mexico. Within a comparatively short time after he married Luz Beaubien, daughter of one of the original grantees, Lucien B. Maxwell became the owner of all the interests in the Grant.

Charles Bent, first governor of New Mexico after the American Occupation, acquired during his lifetime a fractional interest in the Maxwell Land Grant. Just how Governor Bent obtained the interest is a matter of conjecture, but it is known that upon his death his heirs at law claimed that he had procured an undivided one-third interest by a parol agreement, presumably made with Beaubien and Miranda, original owners of the Grant. The district court of Taos County at its May term in 1865, with Judge Kirby Benedict on the bench, found, however, that Charles Bent in his lifetime had owned only an undivided one-fourth interest in the Grant. A compromise was effected by Lucien B. Maxwell, and by court decree, whereby a valuation of eighteen thousand dollars was placed upon the undivided one-fourth interest. The money was ordered to be paid to Alfred Bent, Estefena Bent Hicklin and Teresa Bent Scheurich, children of Charles Bent. Alfred Bent died suddenly in 1866 and Guadalupe Bent, his widow, who later married George W.

Thompson, began litigation to set aside the decree of the court fixing the valuation, alleging fraud and undue influence on the part of Lucien B. Maxwell in having her appointed guardian ad litem for her minor children, Charles Bent, Alberto Silas Bent and Juliano Bent, and in inducing her as administratix of the estate of her deceased husband, Alfred Bent, to execute papers in connection with the transfer of her late husband's interests in the Grant. The litigation turned largely on technicalities and in the final decisions the Bent children lost out and Lucien B. Maxwell eventually acquired all of the Bent interests.*

Guadalupe Miranda, undoubtedly the author of the petition addressed to Governor Manuel Armijo, in Santa Fe, on January 8, 1841, asking for a grant of land, which was also signed by Carlos Beaubien, apparently never realized the extent or value of the property that had been granted to him. The only available record of Miranda's thoughts in regard to the Grant is a letter written on February 24, 1858 from Franklin, the present El Paso, Texas, addressed to Charles Beaubien. The letter reveals that Miranda was a man of education and of sensitive character.† The letter, somewhat pathetic, in the light of subsequent events, when Lucien B. Maxwell received for the grant such a large sum of money, is as follows:

"Franklin, Feb'y. 24, 1858.
"Mr. Charles Beaubien:
"I have written to you several times but have not received any answer, and I infer that mine have not

---

* See Bent vs. Maxwell Land Grant & Ry. Co., 3 N. M. 159; Thompson v. Maxwell Land Grant & Ry. Co., 3 N. M. 269; 95 U. S. 391; Charles Bent v. Guadalupe Miranda, 8 N. M. 78; Maxwell Land Grant & Railway Co. v. Guadalupe Thompson, 8 N. M. 91.

† Guadalupe Miranda was Secretary of the Mexican Departmental Government in Santa Fe, and in 1841 carried on an extensive correspondence with Manuel Alvarez, United States Consul at Santa Fe, in Mexico. Alvarez had been appointed Consul by the State Department March 22, 1839. Guadalupe Miranda taught young men the elements of Spanish grammar, Latin, and the rudiments of philosophy at a school established in the home of Vicar General Don Juan Rafael Rascon in Santa Fe in the early part of the 19th century.

Peter Maxwell and Henry J. Leis

been received by you. Circumstances place men in different positions, sometimes favorable and at others unfavorable. In the latter condition I find myself, and my circumstances are such as to oblige me to do that which at other times I would not do. Thrust out from my country, a portion of my property abandoned, and the rest for a year and months at the disposition of my enemies, my resources have been reduced to such a degree that today, in order to maintain my numerous family, I find myself obliged to dispose of that which remains to me, through the favor of friends like yourself. Don Pablo Miranda, my son, will visit you and sell you the part of land which belongs to me of our premises on the Red River. Our deceased friend, Don Carlos, proposed to buy it. I had no intention to sell, for from the beginning I reserved this property for my sons as New Mexicans. Today, circumstances compel me to this course, as an only recourse. This is the reason. Why should I conceal it? Gentlemen have spoken to me in regard to the matter, but I have not considered it proper to sell without seeing you first, as partner and friend. So, if you do not wish to purchase my part, then I will sell to another, of those who seek to purchase. Therefore, my son, Don Pablo Miranda, is empowered by me to sell, contract, and settle with you the business fully, and with ample power to dispose of my part in his discretion, as legitimate owner.

Your affectionate friend, who respects you, and kisses your hand,
GUADALUPE MIRANDA."

Charles Beaubien did not purchase the interest of Guadalupe Miranda, but Lucien B. Maxwell did, for on April 7, 1858, L.

Pablo Miranda, in the presence of Fred Muller and Charles Beaubien, executed a "transfer of title," as agent for Guadalupe Miranda, whose residence was given as El Paso, in the state of Chihuahua, and Republic of Mexico. Maxwell's residence was given as County of Taos, Territory of New Mexico. The consideration passing from Maxwell to L. Pablo Miranda was one thousand dollars in United States money, a note for one thousand dollars additional to be paid on July 1, 1858, an additional sum of five hundred dollars to be paid when the Congress of the United States should pass favorably on the Beaubien-Miranda claim; and the sum of two hundred forty-five dollars to be paid to Charles Beaubien for expenses paid by him for investigation of the legality of the claim or grant, making the sum total of two thousand seven hundred forty-five dollars. The letter of Guadalupe Miranda of February 24, 1858, was accepted as a power of attorney from him to his son and recorded in Taos County as evidence of his authority to sell. Either L. Pablo Miranda was a poor trader, or his father, Guadalupe Miranda, was in fearfully desperate straits financially, or Lucien B. Maxwell was a hard trader.

Guadalupe Miranda sold his undivided one-half interest in the Grant for less than three thousand dollars. If Miranda had held on to the property for ten years longer and sold out with Lucien B. Maxwell, his one-half of the purchase price would have been three hundred twenty-five thousand dollars. On May 19, 1868, Guadalupe Miranda, in El Paso, state of Chihuahua, Mexico, executed a quitclaim deed to Lucien B. Maxwell for his undivided one-half interest in the Grant, confirming the document his son, L. Pablo Miranda, had executed in New Mexico on April 7, 1858. The execution of the conveyance by Guadalupe Miranda to Lucien B. Maxwell as of May 19, 1868, indicates that Miranda probably lived until after the time Maxwell received the purchase price of $650,000 for the property.

Gradually Lucien B. Maxwell acquired all the outstanding interests in the Grant. On September 14, 1858, Charles Beaubien and Maria Paula Beaubien, his wife, conveyed to Lucien B. Maxwell, for a consideration of five hundred dollars, a tract of land two and one-quarter miles square at Rayado. On April 4, 1864, Lucien B. Maxwell acquired for a consideration of five hundred dollars, the right of Teodorita Beaubien, wife of Fred Muller, which she had acquired from her father, the late Charles Beaubien, deceased, of Taos County. On the same day for a consideration of thirty-five hundred dollars, represented by two promissory notes of $1,750 each, with early maturity dates, Lucien B. Maxwell acquired the interest of Juana Beaubien, wife of Joseph Clouthier. Juana in her deed recited that she was granting her rights as an heir of her father, the late Charles Beaubien, being her undivided interest in the grant, as one of the six heirs of Charles Beaubien. On July 20, 1864, Lucien B. Maxwell acquired the interest of Eleanor Beaubien, wife of Vidal Trujillo, of Mora, Mora County, for a consideration of three thousand dollars in cash. On February 1, 1867, Lucien B. Maxwell acquired for three thousand five hundred dollars the interests of Petra Beaubien Abreu, wife of Jesus G. Abreu, which she had acquired as a daughter of the late Charles Beaubien. The Abreus were residents of "Rallado" (Rayado), Mora County, at the time of the execution of the deed. On January 1, 1870, Paul Beaubien conveyed for thirty-five hundred dollars all the right he had acquired in the Grant from his father, the late Charles Beaubien. On May 3, 1866, Teresina Bent Scheurich, wife of Aloys Scheurich, for a consideration of six thousand dollars, conveyed to Lucien B. Maxwell an undivided one-twelfth interest in the Grant which she had inherited as a child of and one of the heirs of Charles Bent. The Scheurichs obtained a more substantial amount for an undivided one-twelfth interest than several other heirs had obtained for an undivided one-sixth interest.

Altogether, Lucien B. Maxwell did not pay more than fifty

thousand dollars for all of the outstanding interests in the Grant. It is quite probable that at the time the trades were being made for the outstanding interests neither Lucien B. Maxwell nor any of his in-laws or even Guadalupe Miranda knew or understood what the future held for the Grant in the way of acreage. It was freely said in the late sixties and early seventies, and by old timers today, that standing at the old Kit Carson place at Rayado, the calls in the description of the Grant could be plainly seen, and that they called for a modest thirty-two thousand acres of land, using the beginning point, as set forth in the description contained in the original petition, "below the junction of the Rayado River with the Colorado," using as a central point, "the top of the mountain which divides the waters of the rivers running toward the east from those running toward the west," and finally, if vaguely, back, "to the place of beginning."

A patent to the Grant from the United States of America was not issued until May 19, 1879, several years after Maxwell's death. It was issued in the name of Beaubien and Miranda, grantees of the government of Mexico. Legally the beneficial title immediately inured to Maxwell Land Grant Company.

CHAPTER VI

The Indians

FOR YEARS unknown to the white man, the Plains Indians considered as their own the country in New Mexico and southern Colorado identified in modern times as the Maxwell Land Grant. Thousands of the Plains Indians had been killed in inter-tribal wars, in battles with Mexican settlers, American pioneers. Decimated by scourges of smallpox and other devastating diseases, their tribes had dwindled greatly in numbers. The Indians had been pushed back from the Plains country further and further into the interior of New Mexico. For several years prior to 1861, the Muache Utes and the Jicarilla Apaches had wandered about the northeastern part of New Mexico like the Lost Tribes of Israel. They had been kicked from pillar to post by settler and government authority alike.

The relations between the Indians and the people of New Mexico had never been particularly happy under Spanish or Mexican rule and the early decades that followed the American Occupation in 1846 saw but little change. On January 6, 1852, the second Legislature of the Territory of New Mexico adopted a memorial to the Congress of the United States, stating the situation from the viewpoint of the lawmakers. "Since the entrance of the American Army under General Kearney," the memorial recited, "this Territory had been a continual scene of outrage, robbery, and violence, carried on by the savage nations by which it is surrounded; our citizens, both native and adopted, are daily massacred before our eyes, our stock driven from our fields, our property taken from our dwellings, our wives and daughters violated, and our children carried into captivity." Without any attempt to conform to present day spelling, the memorial of 1852 declared, "the presence of the powerful and well armed tribes of the Utahs, Kiaways, Shienes, and Jickorias on the north; the Comanches and Pawnes on the east and southeast; the Mescaleras on the south; and the Gila and Coita Apaches and Navajos on the west and southwest, render it impossible for our citizens, unarmed and impoverished as they are, to resist, avert or prevent these evils."

The Legislature recommended to the federal government a policy of force, a war of extermination, carried on against the Indians by those "who are acquainted with their retreats and mode of warfare." The federal government was asked to permit New Mexico to raise two regiments to be placed in the field and maintained at the expense of the United States to carry the fight to the Indians.

In the year 1861 the remnants of the Muache Utes and Jicarilla Apaches were located on the west side of the Taos Mountain, near Taos. The valley of the Taos in that period was well populated with Pueblo Indians, former citizens of Mexico, and Americans. Whiskey was one of the most important articles of commerce in the Taos area. A brisk trade in that item was carried on with the Utes and Apaches, especially when they made their periodical trips to the Indian agency to receive their presents and supplies, most of which were promptly traded for fire water. The sellers of the whiskey to the Indians could not at that time be reached by law. The result was disastrous to the Indians. The federal authorities apparently believed that to save the Indians from utter extinction it would be best to remove them to the other side of the mountain.

Representatives of the government negotiated with Lucien B. Maxwell, and on March 10, 1862, a twenty-five year lease was entered into between Maxwell and W. F. M. Arny, United

States Indian Agent, on behalf of the government of the United States for twelve hundred acres of land on the Maxwell Grant at an annual rental of twenty dollars. The Utes and Jicarilla Apaches were taken to the Grant and hemmed up in an area that would not make a respectable ranch in New Mexico country for much more than one individual. Two thousand dollars were expended in log and adobe plastered improvements, a schoolroom, cook room and council chamber for the Indians; and a residence of six rooms for the Indian agent and his family.

In the Territory of New Mexico for the years 1848 to 1868, the federal government expended large sums of money in an attempt to subdue the Indians. In the report of J. R. Doolittle, Chairman of the Joint Special Congressional Committee, dated January 27, 1867, it was said:

> "Since we acquired New Mexico, the military expenditures connected with Indian affairs have probably exceeded $4,000,000 annually in that Territory alone. When General Sumner was in command of that department he recommended the purchase of all the private property of citizens and the surrender of the whole Territory to the Indians, and upon the score of economy it would doubtless have been a great saving to the Government."

A most interesting review of the entire Indian situation, so far as it pertained to New Mexico, was given in a letter written in 1843 by Antonio Jose Martinez, curate of Taos, to the Mexican government, directed to General Don Antonio Lopez de Santa Anna. Padre Martinez was very familiar with the Indian situation both before and after the American Occupation. To quote parts of the Padre Martinez letter:

> "It is a true and notorious fact that the wild tribes dwelling in the vicinity, as well as in different parts of

this Department of New Mexico, live by the produce of the chase and robberies, since they neither cultivate the lands nor raise cattle, which is done only by the Navajo tribe, unfortunately the most ferocious and the most faithless in their treaties of peace, whenever they happen to make any . . . It is a fact that the various species of deer and other game which formerly roamed the plains in great quantity, throughout the country north crossing the east to the south, have greatly diminished. It is certain that the buffaloes must greatly diminish. . . . It is the custom of the Apaches and Utes every year, in the autumn to place their huts near the cornfields, and to steal maize and other productions, thus causing important losses to the farmers."

On July 26, 1865, Padre Martinez, writing to J. R. Doolittle, Chairman of the Committee on Indian Affairs in the United States Congress, frankly gave his views on the Indian situation in New Mexico, and with especial reference to the Utes and Jicarilla Apaches, made the following statement:

"The Utas, since I have acquired the use of reason, were always at peace with New Mexico; notwithstanding which they stole and killed some cattle, such as cows and ewes, whenever these happened to be grazing in the pasture lands. But after the year 1843, I am not certain which, some chiefs arrived in the city of Santa Fe to hold an interview with the governor, whose name was Martinez, from the state of Chihuahua. Behaving insolently toward the governor, the troops fired at the Indians and killed one of them. This, to my knowledge, is the first insurrection of the Yutas; but after this, there was another one in New Mexico against the United States government. At

THE INDIANS 49

that time also, there was a revolt of the Apaches, called Jicarillas, who always lived between the villages and the intermediate mountains, working and selling earthenwares to our people. They trespassed upon the lands of the Yutas in the eastern part of the Territory, in search of buffaloes and other game, although they had some in great quantity in their own section of the country. But in this insurrection they were severely punished and soon after they concluded a peace with the Yutas, which exists to the present day."

In connection with the warlike tendencies of Ute and Jicarilla Apache Indians, Padre Martinez said:

"The Indians are always at war with each other. The Yutas have been constantly at war against the nations of the north, and also with the Comanches against whom they already made several campaigns . . . The Apache Jicarillas and those from the south were always at war with the Comanches."*

During the Civil War and for some years after the war, the Indians gave the United States Army a great deal to think about. Brigadier General James H. Carleton was the commanding officer in charge of the Headquarters of the Department of New Mexico at Santa Fe. He frequently conferred with Kit Carson, noted Indian Scout, who had been in New Mexico since 1826, and who knew the Indians intimately, in peace and in war. On November 29, 1864, Kit Carson gave his views about Indian troubles, saying among other things:

* For the Padre Martinez letters see "Report of the Condition of Indian Tribes," published in 1867 by Government Printing Office, pages 358 and 486. For comments on tribal background of Utes, see "Moache Utes," in Hodge's Handbook of American Indians, Part 1, P. 915; and for Bancroft's views of Utes and Jicarilla Apaches, see Bancroft, Vol. 27, Arizona and New Mexico Pp. 666 and 736.

> "I think, as a general thing, the difficulties arise from aggressions on the part of the whites. From what I have heard, the whites are always cursing the Indians, and are not willing to do them justice. For instance, at times large trains come out to this country, and some man without any responsibility is hired to guard the horses, mules and stock of the trains; these cattle by his negligence frequently stray off; always, if anything is lost, the cry is that the Indians stole it. It is customary, among the Indians, even among themselves, if they lose animals, as Indians go everywhere, if they bring them in they expect to get something for their trouble. Among themselves they always pay, but when brought in to this man, who lost them through negligence, he refuses to pay, and abuses the Indians, striking or sometimes shooting them because they do not wish to give up the stock without pay; and thus a war is brought on."

During the sixties, the United States Army in New Mexico announced a war of extermination against the Apaches and Navajos. Bosque Redondo, at Fort Sumner, later home of Lucien B. Maxwell, was the sorry place, of all places, chosen for the future home of the Indians. Apaches were first impounded there, and later the Navajos. At one time some nine thousand Navajos were virtually prisoners at Bosque Redondo.

Speaking of the Jicarilla Apaches and Utes in his statement of November 29, 1864, Col. Kit Carson said:

> "I think the Jicarilla Apaches would object to being put on the Bosque. The Utes know nothing of planting. They are a brave, warlike people; they are of rather small size, but hardy and very fine shots. They are generally hungry, and killing cattle and sheep, which will bring on a war. They are now at peace,

THE INDIANS

and it would be the wiser thing to remain at peace with them."

With his time greatly taken with the prosecution of the major war that was being carried on against the Navajos, and a minor war against the Apaches, both in New Mexico, General Carleton had but little time to devote to the status of the Utes and Jicarilla Apaches, now domiciled on the Maxwell Land Grant. Lucien B. Maxwell, however, was in close contact with these Indians, and learned they were anxious to go on the warpath against their ancient enemies, the Kiowas and Commanches. Maxwell communicated his knowledge to Brigadier General Crocker, with the result that on September 18, 1864, from Santa Fe, General Carleton wrote to Colonel Christopher Carson, 1st Cavalry, New Mexico Volunteers, at Taos, a letter, which said among other things:

"I have received, through Brigadier General Crocker, United States Volunteers, a message from Lucien B. Maxwell, that some two hundred or more Ute Indians, now near Mr. Maxwell's place on the Little Cimarron, are willing and anxious to go out on the plains and attack the Kiowas and other Indians now depredating upon our trains and killing our people who are enroute to and from the states and New Mexico, provided they, the Utes, can be furnished with some rations, ammunition, perhaps a blanket apiece, and provided they may keep whatever stock or other property they may be able to capture from the hostile Indians alluded to."

Sympathetic with the plan, Col. Carson went to Lucien B. Maxwell's ranch and conferred with him, and was authorized by General Carleton, on October 14, 1864, to gather up the Utes and Jicarilla Apaches and issue them rations, but to refuse to issue rations for the families of the Indians, which they had demanded. The Utes and Apaches, with warpaint, assembled at Maxwell's Ranch on October 22, 1864. Minute instructions as to equipment were given by Carleton to Carson. Each Indian in the outfit was to receive one and one-quarter pounds of beef and one pound of breadstuffs per man, and "the necessary salt." The meat and foodstuffs were to be furnished by Lucien B. Maxwell, at government expense, and Carson was to equip his Indian warriors with guns, ammunition, blankets and shirts. Coffee and sugar were to be requisitioned from Fort Bascom.

Carson was given a free hand in the conduct of the expedition against the hostile Kiowas and Comanches and ordered by Carleton to "give them a severe drubbing."

General Carleton said, in a letter to Kit Carson on October 23, 1864: "I need not repeat to you the orders given to all commanders whom I have sent out to fight the Indians, that women and children will not be killed, only men who bear arms."

With his New Mexico troops, aided by the Utes and Jicarilla Apaches, Carson went looking for Plains Indians. He met and defeated the Kiowas on November 25, 1864. Word of the battle was received by General Carleton at Las Cruces, from which place he wrote to Carson at Fort Bascom on December 15, 1864:

> "I beg to express to you and to the gallant officers and soldiers whom you have commanded in your battle with the Kiowas on November 25, as well as to our good auxiliaries, the Utes and Apaches, my thanks for the handsome manner in which you all met so formidable an enemy and defeated him. Please publish an order to this effect. This brilliant affair adds another green leaf to the laurel wreath which you have so nobly won in the service of your country."

After the "severe drubbing," ordered by Carleton, delegations of the Kiowas and Comanches went to Fort Bascom in February, 1865, and talked peace to the army, bringing with them as evidence of good faith three American women and three children, and one Mexican boy stolen from Chihuahua.

For a number of years before gold had been discovered on the Maxwell Land Grant, and before the value of the Grant had increased so greatly, the government of the United States had been importuned to buy the entire property for the Indians. Indian agent after Indian agent had written to the Secretary of the Interior, directing the correspondence to the attention of the Commissioner of Indian Affairs, urging that the Grant be bought for the Indians, but always without result. Indian agents had informally discussed the proposed purchase of the Grant with Maxwell, so that the Indians would have returned to them the land they claimed as their ancestral hunting and fishing grounds, and at one time a price of a few cents an acre had been tentatively agreed upon. In the report of A. B. Norton, Superintendent of Indian Affairs for New Mexico, from Santa Fe, dated August 27, 1867, directed to N. G. Taylor, Commissioner of Indian Affairs, Washington City, D.C.,* specific mention was made of the plight of the "Utahs" and Apaches of the Cimarron, and the possibility of purchase of the Grant by the government. "These Indians have been fed by the military ever since last September," said the Norton report, "because Ex-Commissioner Cooley forbid their being fed by the Indian Department to the extent of $500 per month as I had authorized, and upon his disapproval of my action, I stopped feeding, and they began to steal. General Carleton saying (which is a fact) 'that it was cheaper to feed them than it was to fight them,' authorized their being fed over $3,000 per month, instead of $500 per month, which gave satisfaction at that time. I would respectfully recommend, in behalf of these Indians, the purchase of the Maxwell Grant and in less than one year they

* Report of the Acting Commissioner of Indian Affairs, 1867.

could be made self-sustaining. There is no use avoiding the issue. It is useless to talk of moving them elsewhere; they would resist to the last extremity, and four times the cost of the Grant, $250,000, would be spent in less than one year in fighting to remove them. This is a tract of land 40 by 60 miles, and containing about 1,500,000 acres (about 16 cents per acre). There are from 3,000 to 5,000 acres now under cultivation, well watered, with a good system of irrigation, good stone water mill costing $50,000, a good sawmill and a barn which cost $10,000, good dwelling, store house, and other outbuildings suitable for agency purposes, good water and abundant, and wood and timber handy enough to last for years."

Apparently Col. Kit Carson, noted Indian scout, had been consulted, for Norton in his report continues:

> "Colonel Carson says that the improvements alone cost more than half the amount asked, which if deducted, would reduce the land to less than eight cents per acre, which would make it quite a speculation to the government, independent of getting the most desirable location for these Indians."

The reports of the agents and their recommendations in regard to purchase of the Grant were printed in the annual volumes of the Commissioner of Indian Affairs, but the Government manifested no interest in acquiring the magificent property for the Indians.

In his report to the Commissioner of Indian Affairs, under date of October 10, 1872, Nathaniel Pope, Superintendent of Indian Affairs in New Mexico, writing from Santa Fe to Hon. Francis A. Walker, then Commissioner, at Washington, reported the discontinuance of Cimarron as a regular agency and advised the Commissioner that the Indians had been "discontented and unruly." Indian Agent Pope said, among other things, in his report for 1872:

"During last winter authority was granted at my request, to remove the Muache Utes to the Ute Agency at Tierra Amarilla, and the Jicarilla Apaches to the Mescalero Apache agency at Fort Stanton. Upon representations made to me, I believed the removal could be accomplished in time, and made the request in view of the fact that the majority of citizens of Cimarron, and especially the 'English Company' who owned the land, earnestly desired to be rid of the Indians, whose presence was and is a constant source of trouble, and a cause for a general feeling of insecurity among the people of that neighborhood."

The Pope report continued:

"I am now convinced that Cimarron is not a suitable place for these Indians, and that they are surrounded by influences that render their proper control almost an impossibility. They are becoming very overbearing, and insist that the 'Maxwell Grant' belongs to them, and the Muache Utes refuse to leave it, although it has been sold to the English Company referred to and is being rapidly disposed of to settlers. I have tried several experiments to accomplish the removal, but as yet without result... The Indians at Cimarron have become so unruly of late, in consequence of the absence of anyone with authority to look to their interests that I have placed Mr. R. H. Longwill temporarily in charge, for the purpose of feeding and otherwise caring for them until they can be moved."*

The New Mexico Legislature of 1874 addressed a memorial to the Congress of the United States, citing the condition of the Indians. "The Ute and Jicarilla Apache tribes of Indians, rang-

* Report of Commissioner of Indian Affairs for 1872.

ing over the northern portion of the Territory," the Memorial recited, "formerly supported themselves by hunting, but as the buffalo are now to be found only at great distances, and deer and other game have become very scarce, and the country being settled up, the hunting grounds of the Indians are circumscribed, and their means of support greatly reduced, and they are now almost entirely, and soon will be entirely dependent on the bounty of the government for subsistence." Government assistance was inadequate, the Memorial complained, because "while these Indians have been for a number of years under the care of the government, they have in no wise improved, their intelligence and information have not increased, and they are in no better condition at present than when the government first took charge of them." The Memorial continued: "They are today mere wandering vagabonds, and the only change noticeable in them for some years is a decrease in energy and a greater love of whiskey and idleness. The appropriations made for their support and the food supplied to them by the government are insufficient for their wants, and unfortunately the special agents employed at Cimarron for some time past have failed to acquire the confidence of the Indians, or any authority or control over them."

That the Indians were desperate is indicated in another part of the resolution: "The Indians roam through the country and for subsistence kill the sheep and cattle of the people. These Indians are peaceable and seldom commit acts of violence against the whites, except to castigate persons in charge of herds and those who attempt to prevent their taking such stock as they need."

That the Legislature understood the problems of the Indians was reflected in these words of the Memorial:

> "Depredations of this character are constantly committed, and the loss and annoyance to the people of

northern New Mexico is very great; yet in no instance for several years past, has there been any retaliation. The people almost universally feel friendly towards and sympathize with these unfortunate creatures. When remonstrated with, the Indians say, we are hungry and must eat, our agent cares nothing for us, we cannot understand his talk, we are neglected and abandoned and must take care of ourselves as best we may. Their situation is truly deplorable, and forces compassion even on the part of those who suffer from their depredations, and whose property is taken to satisfy their wants."

The Utes and Jicarilla Apaches, the subject of the Memorial of the New Mexico Legislature in 1874, were not the only people who were causing trouble in northern New Mexico. In the early Seventies, the Comanche Indians, long traders with Indians in New Mexico, bartering buffalo meat and buffalo robes for things they wanted from New Mexico, were being hard pressed by men from Texas. The Texans claimed that the Comanches had driven their cattle from Texas into New Mexico and were slaughtering cows and selling cow meat for buffalo meat. The "Comanche Indian Trade," as it was called, was fast becoming a difficult problem for the Comanches, Texans, New Mexicans.

The "New Mexico Union," published in Santa Fe on October 1, 1872, complained bitterly of the attitude of the Texans and blamed them instead of the Indians. The Union contended that men from Texas, armed with every kind of weapon, were invading New Mexico, rounding up cattle, regardless of brand or ownership, and running them back into Texas on the pretext that they were cattle that had been run out of Texas by the Comanche Indians. They came into New Mexico, the Union complained, "with braggadocio, swaggering and offers of violence."

"Too often these blowing bullies have succeeded with their pretensions," continued the Union. "We say no just, decided, true man, neither under the laws of God or man should allow himself for a moment to be in any manner trampled upon by the disgusting, cowardly pretender. The time has come when people should hold their own rights in their own hands. We repeat our wonder at the submission of a wronged people. For weeks, men in bands from Texas have ranged with pistols, rifles and knives and have taken cattle where they pleased, under the pretense that they had at some time been unlawfully taken from Texas. Is there another country in the United States where the whole community would not rebel at the outrage? We say to the people, take care of your own interests. You have no safety but in your own hands."

In connection with the adoption of the Memorial on the Indian situation by the Legislature of 1874, the lawmakers requested S. B. Elkins, then Delegate in Congress from New Mexico, to present the petition in Washington. Apparently Elkins was not particularly interested in the plight of the Indians. In the seventies Elkins spent months at a time in England and Holland, seeking capital for various enterprises in New Mexico, including a railroad project. His enemies claimed he was abroad to interest moneyed men in the Maxwell Land Grant property. Elkins was at one time an officer of the Maxwell Land Grant and Railway Company.

The Congress of the United States paid scant attention to the legislative memorial of the New Mexico Legislature in 1874. Urgent recommendations continued to be made by Indian agents to those in authority in Washington to do something for the Indians, but without result. Use of the military was urged by those out of sympathy with the Indians and their affairs. Many openly advocated shooting the Indians down, quieting them once and for all. John G. Koogler, editor-lawyer, in the Las Vegas Gazette of October 5, 1872, in a summary of the

Indian situation in northern New Mexico, said that but two courses were open to New Mexico and the federal government, one the use of bullets, the other use of bread and blankets, and he recommended the latter.

In the Fall of 1875 conditions with the Utes and Jicarilla Apaches reached a crisis. The Utes started on a long buffalo hunt, and the Apaches awaited their return. The hunt was not a success, and the Government rations were not to the liking of the Indians. On November 20, 1875, while A. G. Irvine, the Indian Agent at Cimarron, was handing out meat rations, several of the Indians protested and threw the meat back at the agent, claiming it was spoiled. Pistol shots were exchanged, Juan Barela, a minor chief, half Ute, half Jicarilla Apache, was shot and killed, and it appeared probable that the Indians would go on the warpath. Troops hurried over from Cimarron, a few miles from the scene of the trouble. The Indians sent their women and children to places of safety. Captain McCleave, with the reputation of being "one of the oldest and best Indian fighters of the Plains," in command of the federal troops, promised a vigorous policy in dealing with the two tribes. McCleave gave the Indians their choice of either going to their reservations or fighting, and, by way of inducement, stopped their rations until they should come to terms.

General Nelson A. Miles arrived in Cimarron on December 11, 1875, and his acts changed the situation over night. This noted Indian fighter made a quick survey of the facts on the ground. He observed with his own eyes the pitiable condition to which the Indians had been reduced and ordered the immediate resumption of rations. By way of a peace offering General Miles had issued to the Indians chunks of the best beef in town.

By Christmas-time in 1875 both bands of Indians were settled for the winter near Cimarron. General Miles had decided it was too cold to remove them to their reservations. He believed some of the women and chidren might freeze on the journey, and doubted the ability of the agents of the government to care for them after they would reach their destination.

The "Las Vegas Gazette" of December 25, 1875, remarked that "it would pay the territory of New Mexico to provide for the board of these two bands of beggarly poor Indians at some hotel in the east, rather than allow them to remain longer in New Mexico." The Gazette complained that "they have hunted and fished along the mountain streams and eaten government beef until they have lost all energy and are too lazy and helpless to do anything . . . They constitute but a handful of poorly clothed, dirty, disgusting men, women and children and could be transferred to some mountain canyon where they would never be heard from again in this world." The Gazette estimated at this time that there were "only about two hundred fifty men, women and children" in the bands.

The attempt to have the Utes and Jicarilla Apaches live on a part of the Maxwell Land Grant in the manner devised by the government had proved a complete failure. The project was abandoned after sixteen years. The Indians had been unhappy for years. They had refused to remain within the confines of the land that Lucien B. Maxwell had leased to the government for their use. The Grant had been sold from under them. The men in charge of affairs in Washington had failed to grasp the significance of the Grant in its relation to the economic problems then, and later confronting dispossessed Indians and dislocated and dispossessed Spanish-Americans.

On September 30, 1876, the Cimarron agency was discontinued, and the government began to remove the Utes to the northern portion of the Ute reservation in Colorado under the charge of the White River Agency, and the Apaches to the Mescalero Agency in the southern part of New Mexico. The Utes were extremely reluctant to go to Colorado, preferring to remain in New Mexico.

When the government finally decided to abandon the Cimarron agency the census disclosed the number of Utes enrolled was 307, Jicarilla Apaches, 442, a total of 749. The Commissioner of Indian Affairs believed that the aid of the military would be required to remove the Indians and place them in the newly selected reservations. Moving the Indians to new homes proved slow and difficult. Complaints poured into Washington in regard to the conduct of the Indians. S. W. Dorsey, then in the United States Senate, later a resident of New Mexico, complained on October 1, 1877, in a letter addressed to Carl Schurz, Secretary of the Interior, that the Utes and Apaches had become insolent and were annoying settlers. "There is no reservation whatever in the vicinity of Cimarron where these Indians live," wrote Dorsey, "and I believe it is the only instance where Indians who have reservations are permitted to roam at will over a vast area of occupied country and spend their whole time among the settlers." Senator Dorsey contended that the Utes had a reservation in Colorado and that the Jicarilla Apaches belonged on a reservation near Fort Stanton, New Mexico. To quote a paragraph from Dorsey's letter:

> "I believe these two bands of Indians, numbering altogether about seven hundred, are unlawfully permitted to remain in a country owned and occupied by white people, commit more depredations in the way of horse stealing, killing cattle and sheep, than any similar band of Indians in the country. They are most insolent in their demeanor and demands. They will ride up to a settler's house in lots of ten or twenty and order food to be prepared for them; if the settler has not got it, he has to get it. They go into a herd of cattle or sheep in the presence of the owner and kill as many as they want with impunity. I speak of this matter because I have had some personal experience with them this summer, and I think it is due the citizens of that

country, as well as the government, that these Indians be removed to their respective reservations, and trust you will call the attention of Congress to the necessity of doing so."

That the Indians were in a bad way was the report of B. M. Thomas, who was Indian agent for the Pueblos and the Cimarron agency at the same time. In a report from Santa Fe to the Commissioner of Indian Affairs on August 20, 1877, Thomas said:

"The Indians of the Cimarron agency number 749, of this number 307 are Muache Utes and 442 are Jicarilla Apaches. They are all vagabonds, and there is no hope of improving their condition as long as they remain at their present location. They will not go elsewhere until they are compelled to do so by a large military force. They do nothing for their own support except a little hunting. The government gives them a little clothing and other presents, and issues them weekly rations of beef and flour. They have no reservation where they are, and the agency is located in a small country town, where the Indians can usually procure all the whiskey they can pay for."

The ration of flour and beef referred to by Indian Agent Thomas consisted of seven pounds of flour and three and a half pounds of beef per Indian weekly. William Vandever, United States Indian Inspector, made a personal visit to the Cimarron agency and reported to the Commissioner of Indian Affairs on November 15, 1877, that the Utes and Jicarilla Apaches were "non treaty Indians; simply vagrants, trespassing upon lands the title of which has passed from the government." He told the Commissioner that there was an annual issue, generally in the Fall, of blankets, muslin, calico, frying pans and other like articles at the Cimarron Agency, but that the Indians did not show up for the distribution in that year because they "had stampeded to escape the dreaded disease of smallpox." Inspector Vandever recommended forcible removal of the Indians to their reservations, advising the Commissioner that General E. Hatch, Commander of the District, could put them where they belonged without great difficulty and at little cost to the government.

The government officials in Washington, as was usual at the time, a defect perhaps since cured, were somewhat confused on the geography of New Mexico, and unable to understand how Apache Indians were roaming about near Cimarron, when they should be on their reservation near Fort Stanton, some three hundred miles away, not realizing the difference in the situation that existed between the Mescalero Apaches and the Jicarilla Apaches.

A close up view of the Jicarilla Apaches and the Utes about the time they were being put off the Maxwell Land Grant for the last time, written in the free and easy style of a newspaper man, is contained in the "Las Vegas Gazette" for September 30, 1876:

> "That part of New Mexico lying north of the San Juan River and East of the Navajo reservation was at one time set apart for the Jicarilla Apaches. This Tribe was divided into two bands, one having their agency at Cimarron on the east side of the mountains, and the other at Tierra Amarilla, west of the Rio Grande. There are also a couple of bands of Utes who live with these Indians and affiliate with them. The Utes never had a reservation but always laid claim to the same reservation as the Jicarillas. The Jicarilla Apaches would never live on their reservation though often entreated to do so. The chief of the tribe at

Cimarron is San Pablo (Saint Paul), a tall, lantern jawed, but worthy, dignified and peaceably disposed redskin. He has kept the tribe at peace for fourteen years. Aguila (the Eagle) is chief of the band of Utes at Cimarron and like many white men he is inclined to be a warrior when he is drunk. Sober he is good enough. San Pablo knows very well that the mountainous and heavily timbered regions of the streams forming the headwaters of the Canadian River is a much better country for him and his tribe than the valley of the San Juan and the adjacent mesas, barren alike of timber and of game. They do not care for fertile valleys. They prefer to peel the bark in the winter time, from huge pine trees of the forests of the Maxwell Grant, and hunt and fish for a livelihood in the summer than to settle down to a monotonous agricultural life in the fertile valley of the San Juan. Besides, should San Pablo propose to take his tribe to that country they would scalp him in a minute. Thus his wisdom and his fears alike have conjured him to resist the blandishments and presents of the Indian agents and to remain where he is. In this the old Saint shows good sense."

All that portion of New Mexico north of the San Juan River and east of the Navajo reservation was made public land and thrown open to settlement and occupation on August 1, 1876, when President U. S. Grant, by proclamation, abrogated the treaty with the Jicarilla Apaches and declared the land open to settlement by citizens of the United States. The lands were opened to settlement under the belief that the lands set apart for the tribe were not at all suited to the life of uncivilized tribes, and because the Indians had never occupied the reservation as a tribe since its establishment.

Continued application of pressure, mostly by the new owners of the Maxwell Land Grant, finally resulted in the removal of the Utes and Jicarilla Apaches to reservations, where, under the guidance of understanding Indian agents, they worked out their destinies, somewhat along the lines suggested in the New Mexico Legislative Memorial of 1874. The two tribes left the Cimarron country, however, protesting to the last that the Maxwell Land Grant was their property and that they were being wrongfully ejected from their ancestral home. The federal government, claiming the Indians as wards of the government, had failed to grasp the opportunity to purchase from Lucien B. Maxwell for sixteen cents an acre his Grant of almost two million acres, thus overlooking a magnificent opportunity to rehabilitate them, their kinsmen and neighbors who had been under the belief for generations that the Grant country was their property.*

* The fight with the Kiowas on November 25, 1864, in which Kit Carson led the Utes and Jicarilla Apaches is identified as the First Adobe Walls fight. Kit Carson was described by Maurice Trauer, residing in Fort Stanton in 1862, and later a resident of Las Vegas, as being about five feet eight inches in height, always dressed rather commonly, clean shaven face, light hair and light gray eyes, with a quiet manner of speaking, and a slouchy walker. Carson, according to Trauer, smoked, drank and played poker, all in moderation, and carried a clear head into every emergency. Carson's great influence with the Indians, Trauer said, resulted from the fact that Carson always kept any promise or pledge he made to them. See Lincoln County Leader April 13, 1882. For an interesting first hand account of the Adobe Walls Fight see Historical Society of New Mexico, No. 12, "Personal Narratives of the Battles of the Rebellion—Kit Carson's Fight with the Comanche and Kiowa Indians, by Capt. George H. Pettis, First Regiment of Infantry, California Volunteers."

CHAPTER VII
The Cimarron Country

IN the seventies and eighties, that part of New Mexico within a radius of fifty miles of Cimarron was as interesting and as picturesque as any in the West. There adventure beckoned, there glamor and romance lured, there splendor of accomplishment was rewarded by the accolade fate reserves for men of destiny. The town of Cimarron was not too far away by horseback or stage coach from Fort Union, Taos, Elizabethtown, Rayado, Red River, Ocate, Mora or Las Vegas. Lucien B. Maxwell, while he owned the Maxwell Land Grant, with his places of residence at Rayado and Cimarron, set the pace for hospitality. Cimarron was the heart of an immense country that lured trappers, buffalo hunters, cattle growers, Indians, soldiers, prospectors and adventurers. Rival wild west shows were exhibiting their attractions in New Mexico, notably the Lincoln County War in the southwestern part of the Territory, which culminated in the shooting of William H. Bonney, "Billy the Kid," on July 14, 1881, and the Rio Arriba County War, in the northwestern part of New Mexico, where the government had pushed the Indians out to make way for white settlers—only to find that Port Stockton and Ike Stockton and their gangs had something to say about how a new country should be settled up. Cimarron, however, had more than other New Mexico towns to offer those seeking color, romance and adventure. The discovery of gold on the Maxwell Land Grant was the signal for a great rush into the area. The stampede of men built Elizabethtown, Red River and other mining towns almost over night. At one time during the mining boom ten thousand people could be counted in the mining camps of Elizabethtown and Red River, most of them men, from every state in the Union and from foreign countries.

Sunday was the big day in the seventies, when things were uproaring. The Railway Press & Telegraph of Elizabeth City, of March 15, 1873, gave in detail the programs for horse racing, cock fighting, preaching, a wedding and a grand fandango at Garrick's Hall. The program for the Sabbath Day somewhat shocked the editor of the Las Vegas Gazette, which printed an editorial suggesting that missionaries be sent to the Cimarron country to convert the heathen. Newspapers and their editors were obliged to take a chance along with everybody else in the affairs of the day. On January 21, 1876, a newspaper published at Cimarron, with the high sounding name of "Cimarron News and Elizabeth City Railway Press and Telegraph," met with rather a tragic reversal. The paper was published by Will D. Dawson, and the masthead carried the names of three editors, Will D. Dawson, W. R. Morley and Frank W. Springer. Editorials were written, apparently without much consideration, because readers could not with any degree of assurance match up editor and editorial. Clay Allison, noted bad man of the Cimarron country, "and associates," as he later explained, visited the newspaper office on that date in the night time. Clay Allison had taken offense at something that had been written about him. The press, type and equipment of the office were taken out and thrown into the Cimarron River. Somehow, and someway, Publisher Will D. Dawson, true to newspaper tradition, got out a four-page paper on January 28, 1876, with news items only on the front and back pages. The inside bore the legend, "Earthquake—postponed." There was also the following explanation:

"Since the last issue, our forms and type are knocked into 'pi,' and for the most part totally ruined, as is also the press; but though the loss is heavy we will soon be able to present you with a paper as large and well printed as before."

The Cimarron News and Press, however, suspended publication permanently on September 15, 1876.

The sheriff of Colfax County, and all his deputies, were of necessity men who had made out their last wills and testaments and had otherwise arranged their worldly affairs. They could not tell at what particular moment they might be asked to seek refuge in another world. On May 21, 1876, the same day on which Clay Allison in Cimarron shot and killed Pancho Griego, David Crockett, a nephew of the original David Crockett, and his companion, Gus Heffron, shot and killed three negro soldiers from Fort Union. The three negroes came into Cimarron from the Fort and camped below the old St. James Hotel, owned and operated by Henry Lambert. The negroes went to the bar and insisted that Lambert serve them liquor. Lambert told them he would sell them liquor in flasks and they could take it outside and do their drinking. Crockett and Heffron became involved in the argument that ensued. Crockett started to shoot. The negroes were unable to get at their six shooters quickly because of an army issued metal device which held side arms to cartridge belts. When the smoke cleared away, the three negroes, John Black, Charles Morris and Pomeron W. Laughlin, were dead. Three bullets were found lodged in each body. A quarrel then arose in the town saloons about where the negroes should be buried and whether markers should be placed at the head or foot of the graves. The men were finally buried in the Cimarron cemetery. David Crockett and George Heffron were freed on the charge of murdering Black, Morris and Laughlin, on the usual self defense plea, but did not long remain out of trouble. Crockett, ordinarily a peaceful stockman, living on the Vermejo, was shot and instantly killed by a sheriff's posse in Cimarron on October 1, 1876, and at the same time his companion, Heffron, was badly wounded. Crockett and Heffron had come into Cimarron, had become boisterous, refused to quiet down at the command of Sheriff I. Rinehart, who summoned a posse which attempted to arrest the two men. It was claimed they resisted arrest. When the shooting was over for the moment, David Crockett was a corpse and Heffron badly hurt. The Las Vegas Gazette of October 7, 1876, commenting on the affair, said:

> "Crockett and Heffron had been good citizens, but they got it into their heads they should act as desperadoes and outlaws; they would get drunk and ride through the streets of Cimarron, enter stores and even private dwellings, riding horseback, break showcases in stores, compel clerks to black their boots at point of shotgun and pistol. Finally Sheriff Rinehart and the posse got tired of the foolishness. Crockett was given a respectable burial when he was killed. Heffron was treated by a doctor and placed in jail."

Henry Lambert, one of the leading citizens of the town of Cimarron, and who owned and operated the St. James Hotel, gathering place for the entire country, was a picturesque character. His hotel was the place where the stage coaches stopped and drivers and passengers had their lay over, and where soldiers and officers from Fort Union stopped when off duty and on furloughs. Lambert was born October 28, 1838, died on January 24, 1913. He had been a cook in the field for Gen. U. S. Grant during the Civil War and later cooked in the White House for President Abraham Lincoln. He drifted west looking for gold on the Maxwell Land Grant during the final months of the Civil War, reached Elizabethtown in 1864, where he remained for several years, building the present St. James (San Diego) Hotel, in Cimarron in 1880.

The fast stage coach that ran between the end of the railroad in Colorado and Santa Fe had Cimarron as one of its important stops. The Overland Mail & Express, as it was called, charged passenger rates of twenty cents a mile, but the people grinned and paid it, as for the most part they had no alternative. The stage owners said the price of travel was justified because of the wear and tear on vehicles and animals. However, all was not perfect with stage coach transportation. The Las Vegas Gazette of February 28, 1875, had a few words to say about the Mail &Express, and its owners, Barlow, Sanderson & Co., in regard to conditions on the run from Las Animas to Santa Fe:

> "We might excuse them from being behind time on account of the bad state of the roads," commented the Gazette, "but when passengers have to get out and walk mile after mile to relieve the poor jades they call horses, or when the drivers have to leave the coach on the road and walk on foot to the next station to fetch fresh animals, the broken down horses not being able to pull the coach from one station to another, as frequently happens, staging is a farce."

Educationally, New Mexico, in 1875, according to reports compiled by W. G. Ritch, Secretary of the Territory, was not in any too flourishing a condition. Ritch's report shows that there were 128 public schools in the Territory, with 143 teachers and 5,420 pupils. In forty of the schools English and Spanish were taught. There were in addition 31 private schools, in 21 of which both languages were taught, with a total of 998 pupils. There were also 8 Pueblo Indian schools with 10 teachers and 170 scholars. There were 10 institutions of secondary instruction, with about 45 teachers and 400 scholars.

During 1875 the military forces in New Mexico were under the command of the Department of Missouri, with Companies

"L" and "M" of the Eighth Cavalry stationed at Fort Union. Company "D" was stationed at Fort Stanton, Company "C" at Fort Wingate, Company "I" at Fort Bayard and Company "H" at Fort Selden. The Regimental Flag, an army paper published at Santa Fe, said there were at the time fourteen companies of the regular army in Santa Fe, in all about one thousand men.

The Kansas Pacific Railroad had been built into Las Animas in 1875, the Atchison, Topeka & Santa Fe had been built into Granada. All travel roads united at Fort Union or at Las Vegas, and thence roads branched to Santa Fe, Fort Bascom, Fort Stanton. The stage line from Las Animas to Santa Fe was controlled by Barlow, Sanderson & Co., the line south from Santa Fe was owned by Numa Raymond, of Paraje, on the Rio Grande, with a branch line to Silver City and El Paso, owned by Col. J. F. Bennett, of Silver City.

Enough time had elapsed since the death of Kit Carson, the famous Indian scout, to permit the newspapers of the day to criticize the lack of respect to his memory. The Las Vegas Gazette of February 12, 1876, relying on an exchange, complained that, "while a lot of sergeants and colonels of the late war now have costly marble statues erected to their memory, the body of Kit Carson, the true pathfinder of the Rocky Mountains is being allowed to rest in the low, low ground without anything to mark his grave from the common mounds of prairie dogs." The Rocky Mountain Herald, a Denver publication, was particularly vehement, saying:

> "Kit Carson, the grand old pathfinder—who showed and told Tom Benton, Fremont and the government all they ever knew about this trans-Missouri empire —he who as a frontiersman, Indian fighter and pacificator, explorer, and latterly general of volunteers— who deserved immeasureably of the west—he, we regret to acknowledge, now lies chucked away in a

Luz Beaubien Maxwell

Kit Carson Home at Rayado

coyote patch, under the shade of a couple of cottonwoods on the Arkansas in southern Colorado, without even a piece of picket railing to protect his grave from the prowling wolves, or even a pencil mark on a shingle for a head stone, to tell the traveler that Kit Carson sleeps beneath it. Thus has his grave been allowed to stand, near the public road side, unprotected and unlettered, ever since his sudden death there in 1868, to the shame, not only of Southern Colorado, but all of Colorado and New Mexico also, including the legislatures of both, who are alike ignominiously at fault for it. Valor and fame have few incentives when the bones of such pioneers of bravery as Kit Carson are allowed to lie as they are, while many mere scalawags of the period are honored with monuments to their chance achievements."

The editors of the Las Vegas Gazette and the Rocky Mountain Herald were quickly corrected by the Las Animas Leader which said that "Kit Carson's grave is no longer amid sequestered shades of Boggville on the Arkansas. He was only temporarily interred there. The remains were removed in the Fall of 1868 to Taos, New Mexico, Carson's home."

During 1879 and 1880, the Las Vegas and Vinita Mail and Express Line, owned by J. H. Teats, ran daily buckboards from Las Vegas via La Liendre, Chaperito, Gallinas, Cobra, La Cinta, San Hilario and Fort Bascom. C. B. Austin owned the line that ran daily from Fort Bascom to Fort Elliott. Passengers and express leaving Las Vegas on Tuesday morning were forwarded on the weekly buckboard through to any point in the Panhandle of Texas. Tascosa, a neighboring town, over in the Texas Panhandle, not so far from Cimarron, boasted of two stores, carrying large stocks of goods, a blacksmith shop, drug store, two good physicians, a minister of the gospel, a good church, two good hotels, one billiard room and enough saloons to accommodate all who thirsted after liquor. As late as 1884, the mail route from Las Vegas to Vinita, Indian Territory, now Oklahoma, was still in operation. The total expense to the federal government on the route for nearly three years was three hundred thousand dollars and the revenue for the same period was about five hundred dollars. The route was about 725 miles long, with scarcely any postoffices on the route, and parts of it through the wilderness. Sometimes, according to the Las Vegas Gazette of April 12, 1884, there would not be a single letter in the stage mail bag.*

* The word "Cimarron," locally in Spanish means wild, untamed, and was also used to designate Rocky Mountain Sheep, known to New Mexicans as "carnero cimarron."

CHAPTER VIII
Ministers of the Gospel

DESPERADOES, outlaws, peace officers and men who were neither outlaws nor peace officers, but just ordinary citizens, all had their troubles in the early days of the Maxwell Land Grant. Cimarron, Red River, Elizabethtown and other towns in the Grant area attracted men of all types and characters. Even clergymen were not exempt from the circumstances of the day. Soon after the close of the Civil War, Rev. Thomas Harwood, a one-man army of the Lord, arrived in northern New Mexico and spent his days and years in the service of the Methodist Episcopal Church. He and his fellow ministers preached the gospel to all who would listen, but at times few would hear or heed. There was the talk of gold discoveries on the land grant, excitement incident to acquiring land for ranches and homesteads, the turmoil that was present because of the presence of nearby Fort Union. Liquor, dance halls and gambling houses helped mightily to lure men from the atmosphere of religion.

Murder and sudden death were no novelty in the Grant area, but the murder of a minister of the gospel was something of a sensation. Rev. T. J. Tolby, a Methodist minister, who rode the circuit between Cimarron and Elizabethtown, was found murdered on September 14, 1875, at a place about twenty miles from Cimarron on the Elizabethtown road. The minister's horse was found tied to a tree some three hundred yards from his body, the saddle nine hundred yards away in another direction. Robbery was not the motive because Rev. Tolby's personal effects were intact, his horse, saddle and outfit not stolen.

Immediately following the discovery of the body, anti-grant men charged the murder to Grant men, because the minister had on numerous occasions strongly expressed the view that the Grant belonged to the Indians. He had even gone so far as to begin negotiations for the purchase of a large tract of land along the Vermejo, in Colfax County, as the first step in a program to help rehabilitate the Utes and Apaches.

Governor S. B. Axtell, of the Territory of New Mexico, offered a reward of $500.00 for the apprehension and conviction "of the perpetrator of the dreadful crime of the murder of Rev. T. J. Tolby," but the reward was never claimed. The murderer was never apprehended. Buried with honors of the Masonic Lodge in Cimarron, eulogized by a young lawyer, Frank W. Springer, later to become famous in the Maxwell Land Grant fight on the side of the owners, the murder of Rev. Mr. Tolby continued to be the subject of penetrating inquiry. Rev. O. P. McMains, a fellow minister of the gospel, was greatly affected by Rev. Mr. Tolby's death. He dropped his work for a time as a preacher and turned detective. From clews obtained, McMains was confident that Cruz Vega had killed Tolby. McMains' suspicions enmeshed him in a chain of situations which brought him to trial for murder, caused the sudden death of three men and precipitated much trouble for the church with which he was affiliated.

On October 1, 1875, two weeks and a day after Tolby had been found murdered, the body of Cruz Vega was found hanging to a telegraph pole, about three quarters of a mile north of the Ponil River, in Colfax County, about a mile and a half north of Cimarron. The taut lariat about the neck of Cruz Vega told the story grimly enough. He had been lynched and had been badly treated before being strung up. Bunches of hair had been torn from his scalp and he had been tortured in other ways.

Bit by bit the story of the lynching of Cruz Vega came to

light and the Rev. O. P. McMains was pointed out as the man principally responsible for his death. McMains was arrested for the murder of Cruz Vega, tried before a jury in Mora County District Court on a change of venue from Colfax County, on August 23 and 24, 1877. Col. William Breeden, Attorney-General for the Territory, prosecuted the case for the people, and Frank Springer of Cimarron and Judge William D. Lee of the Vermejo, represented the defendant. The jury was composed of Pedro Morris, Juan Ortega, Benjamin Loewenstein, Concepcion Trujillo, Noverto Saavedra, Nestor Maes, Sacramento Cashmore, Jose Maes Carenias, George W. Scroggins, George Cashmore, Candelaria Bustes and Julian Solis. McMains was found guilty "in the fifth degree," and fined three hundred dollars. Henry L. Waldo, the trial judge, set aside the verdict, which read: "We, the jury find the defendant guilty in the fifth degree and assess the penalty at three hundred dollars." Judge Waldo held that the verdict did not say of what the defendant had been found guilty. McMains was to go to trial again, but the case was dismissed at Taos by Judge Samuel Parks on April 1, 1878. The Las Vegas Gazette, in commenting on the case in its issue of April 6, 1878, said:

> "The case against Rev. O. P. McMains for the murder of Cruz Vega was dismissed at Taos by Judge Samuel Parks. The Legislature repealed the law attaching Colfax to Taos County for judicial purposes, and under which law the indictment was found. This rendered the indictment null and void and consequently the case was easily disposed of. The true situation is that under the evidence McMains could not properly be convicted of murder. The instructions of Judge Waldo at Mora were a virtual acquittal."

Testimony at the trial of McMains at Mora developed many interesting facts. Isaiah Rinehart testified that McMains had asked him to induce Cruz Vega to meet McMains and answer questions that he proposed to ask him in connection with the death of Tolby. McMains had told Rinehart, he testified, that he had interviewed "all the people and they were certain that Vega was implicated in the murder of Rev. Tolby." Rinehart was either unwilling or unable to arrange for the interview, but William Low, a resident in the Moreno Valley, succeeded in employing Cruz Vega to watch his corn fields at night, using that as a pretext for an interview by McMains. By prearrangement, a lighted bonfire in Low's corn field was to be a signal for a group of men to gather. McMains had the idea, so Rinehart testified, that if he and a crowd of men showing force could interview Vega, they could get him to confess to the murder of Tolby, or tell who had killed him. At the signal of the lighted bonfire, a group of men gathered, with McMains present to do the interrogating. McMains attempted to direct the men in their work, but the crowd got out of hand, began to make short work of Vega and finally lynched him.

McMains remained at Low's house during the night, and got up crying, showing signs of great distress. "What is the matter now, Mr. McMains?" was Low's testimony. "Did you hear that shooting last night?" asked McMains. "I came away last night when I found out that I had no control over those men," continued McMains.

The men in the lynching party were all disguised, according to Low, and McMains was wearing a disguise, but disclosed his identity when one of the men in the crowd asked him to step forward.

Cruz Vega at the interview, before being lynched, denied all responsibility for the murder of Tolby, but declared that a man named Manuel Cardenas might know something about it, and that was all he could tell them.

The mere mention by Cruz Vega of the name Manuel Cardenas proved an unfortunate circumstance for that gentleman. The "Vigilantes," as they called themselves, waited patiently until November 10, 1875, for the return of Manuel Cardenas. The mob waylaid him, shot him to death. No public sympathy was forthcoming when Cardenas was assassinated. Newspapers of the day explained that "Cardenas had a bad reputation; that at one time he had been sentenced for murder, and only a short time before he was killed, had been publicly whipped in the Plaza of Taos."

The lynching of Cruz Vega, however, was a different matter. Vega was well known in the community of Cimarron, was serving as a constable of Cimarron precinct at the time of his death. On November 1, 1875, Francisco Griego, commonly called "Pancho," made strong threats against certain people in Cimarron because of the lynching of Vega, to whom he had been related. Griego talked and made threats in the presence of R. C. (Clay) Allison at the St. James Hotel. Allison had nothing whatever to do with the Vega lynching, but promptly shot and killed Griego, when the latter insisted, as Allison claimed, on quarreling with him. Allison had shot two bullets in killing Griego, then ran everybody out of the bar of the St. James Hotel. The bar was locked up and Griego's body was not released to relatives until the next day. The shooting of Griego by Allison in Cimarron was merely a passing incident in the life of R. "Clay" Allison. Nothing was done to him because of the death of "Pancho" Griego.

During the Civil War Clay Allison had gone into the Confederate Army in Tennessee as a boy and a private, and had come out a man and an officer, tradition says, a captain. Whether private or captain, Clay Allison was destined to carve for himself, not only notches in his gun in New Mexico and southern Colorado, but a place in the affairs of Southwestern gunmen. Clay Allison, accompanied by his brother, John Allison, trailed a large number of cattle from the Texas Panhandle, where they had gone after leaving Tennessee, into the attractive grass-land country of Colfax County, New Mexico.

The Allison brothers had never heard of the Maxwell Land

Grant, of Miranda and Beaubien, or Lucien B. Maxwell. They saw a mighty country, with rivers racing down from mountain sides, with springs gushing abundant water from high hills. They saw grass that reminded them of the grass that grew on the hill sides of their native Tennessee. Here was a country worth while at long last. The Allison brothers camped on the Maxwell Grant at a place of their choice, called it a ranch, turned their cattle out to graze, and woe to those who questioned their rights, or asked to see leases or titles. "Grant-men," so-called because they were in opposition to those claiming to own and control the Maxwell Land Grant, were quick to recognize in the Allisons men who were lightning-fast on the draw, who had the voice of authority, the courage to back up a command. Clay Allison enjoyed the atmosphere of Cimarron. The town was wide open, there was plenty of hard liquor and plenty of action. Clay Allison liked liquor, craved action. Brother John Allison was quiet, unassuming, but had the reputation of being a cooler man, and a better shot than Clay. Although John Allison disliked to pick a quarrel, he would stick to the end to see a fight through. The Allisons played a lone hand in the cattle business. They were capable cowmen and their neighbors respected them.

On December 30, 1876, Clay Allison and John Allison went from Cimarron to Las Animas, Colorado, and attended a dance in the Olympic dance hall. Town Marshal Chas. Feber learned of their presence in Las Animas, immediately went to the dance hall and asked them to surrender their guns for the evening. The Allisons politely refused. Feber went out of the hall and soon returned with a shotgun. In the gunplay that followed, both Allisons fired at the same instant. Marshal Feber fell, mortally wounded, but as he was dying, pulled the trigger of his shotgun, wounding John Allison. The Allisons continued to fire bullets into the lifeless body of Marshal Feber. As Clay went over to the slumping body of his brother, he dragged Feber's body with him, and cried out: "John here's the man who shot you. Look at the damned son of a bitch. I killed him." Sheriff Spiers and a posse arrested the Allison brothers shortly after the shooting. Clay assumed all the blame, but claimed he shot in self-defense. The grand jury convened on March 31, 1877, but refused to indict him, and Clay Allison returned to his ranch in Colfax County near the town of Otero. The Santa Fe New Mexican of December 8, 1878, described Clay Allison as a "half breed Indian," and claimed that during the Civil War he was a leader of bushwhackers in Tennessee, "where he plundered union and rebel alike."

Rev. O. P. McMains, finally free from the difficulties that had surrounded him because of his zeal in attempting to ferret out the murderer of his late Brother Tolby, returned to his affiliation with "anti-grant" men on the Maxwell Land Grant. McMains was one of the most fearless, persistent and relentless fighters on the side of the anti-grant men. He carried his fight from protest meetings in New Mexico to the Congress of the United States. By nature a crusader and an intense partisan, McMains took over the fight against the Grant owners as an agent for settlers and squatters, was elected to the New Mexico Legislature. He had settled on some land of the Grant himself and was personally interested in defeating the claims of the Grant company. At last, however, after litigation that lasted for years, McMains was ejected through court decree from his ranch on the Grant. The Sheriff of Colfax County, with execution in hand, gathered up McMains' horses and cattle to satisfy a judgment for costs of the litigation and in connection with the eviction. The Sheriff advertised the livestock for sale. On the day of the sale, fifty ranchers and cowboys attended, formed a ring around the livestock, cocked their revolvers and held their rifles loosely across the pommels of saddles. The leader of the cowboys told the Sheriff, crying the sale, that they were going to kill the first man who made an offer. No offers being made, a cowboy stepped forward, gun in hand, opened the corral gate where the livestock had been impounded for the sale, and turned them out on the open range. The cowboys then gathered the cattle and horses together, restored them to friends of McMains, who kept them for him. McMains was finally obliged to leave the premises involved in the ejectment suit, and found out, as the Indians and Spanish-Americans had found out before him, that he had no ownership of any part of the Maxwell Land Grant.

The McMains' execution sale was the culmination of the war he had carried on against the Grant people for many years. McMains had openly charged that the Secretary of the Interior, John W. Noble, had "wrongfully refused to enforce the valid order of the Department of the Interior of January 28, 1874, requiring lands claimed by The Maxwell Land Grant claimants to be treated as public lands," and claimed that "this wrongful procedure of the Secretary of the Interior," was in the interest of a conspiracy in 1877, of Hon. S. B. Elkins, then a delegate in Congress from New Mexico, and of Hon. T. B. Catron, then United States Attorney for New Mexico, and Hon. J. A. Williamson, then Commissioner of the General Land Office, "to defeat the enforcement of said valid order of January 28, 1874, and to deprive homestead and preemption settlers of private and vested rights, without due process of law, and to defraud the United States of its surveyed land by prosecuting anew the adjudicated Maxwell Claim against the United States in violation of Section 5498 of the Revised Statutes." McMains in an affidavit filed with the Committee on Public Lands on May 9, 1892, claimed that the Secretary of the Interior and the Commissioner of Public Lands were "aiding and abetting by trick and fraud," the conspiracy of Elkins, Catron and Williamson, and "were shielding them, as far as in them lies, the aforesaid conspirators, from the punishment at least of exposure and consequent dishonor and disgrace."*

*Report, Com. Private Lands, 52nd Congress, 1st Session, No. 1824, accompanying Mis. Doc. 305 July 9, 1892.

CHAPTER IX
Anti-Grant Litigation

DIFFICULTIES, financial and otherwise, attended the affairs of the Maxwell Land Grant for many years after Lucien B. Maxwell and Luz Beaubien Maxwell signed their names to documents transferring the title to The Maxwell Land Grant & Railway Company, a corporation originally financed through British pounds sterling and Dutch guilders. From the technical side of the ownership of the Grant, there was a procession of corporations, reincorporations, mortgages, deeds of trust, new officers and directors, new policies, foreclosures, tax sales, endless, interminable, expensive litigation.

From the standpoint of settlement on the Grant, and colonization, British and Dutch overlords never visualized the project in its true setting, never understood that a colony in New Mexico could not be anything like a colony in other parts of the world. The Grant lands were at all times in competition with lands both in the Territory of New Mexico and in adjoining states, open to entry and free homestead. Grandiose efforts of the company to stock the Grant with foreign breeds of horses, cattle and sheep were finally abandoned, notwithstanding availability of ideal grazing and pasture lands in great quantities.

In time anti-grant troubles, including sharp-shooting at the title to the Grant by squatters and their sympathizers, coupled with business and financial mismanagement on the part of the Company, resulted in a bogging down of the entire enterprise. In attempts to evict the squatters from the Grant, the Maxwell Land Grant & Railway Company first sent out polite notices to vacate, then filed ejectment suits in the courts. The settlers retaliated by holding mass meetings, organizing, electing officers, devising ways and means of defense as they termed it of "their lands and homes." A "Squatters' Club" was organized in Cimarron and the first meeting was publicly advertised for four o'clock on April 5, 1873. The meeting was billed as "an anti-land grant public mass meeting." The public mass meeting had been preceded by a meeting of settlers on March 30, 1873, at which it was decided to raise funds to carry on a suit "to test the validity of the Maxwell Land Grant & Railway Company's title to what they claim of the public domain." Officers elected were Joseph Holbrook, chairman, Cimarron; Thomas Martin, Elizabethtown; Edward Wittford, Canadian Ranch; John Hendelong, Cimarron; Jesus Maria Arellano, Cimarron. All "patriotic people of this county are asked to subscribe according to their means for the conducting of said suit," was the notice published following the meeting of March 30, 1873. The meeting of April 5, 1873, at Cimarron was only one of many meetings held on various parts of the Grant. The meetings continued to be held at various times for years, until the final word had been said in the squabble over the Grant and its title, by the Supreme Court of the United States.

The anti-grant cause was of particular moment in Raton. There the Grant and anti-Grant fight flowered in all its bitterness. In the anti-grant contingent, there were two groups, one led by men who believed emphatically in the assistance of Winchester rifles and Colt's revolvers; the other led by Rev. O. P. McMains, a combination preacher and printer, who believed in prayer, in public sentiment, in the printed word. Rev. Mr. McMains, with his Cruz Vega troubles behind him, in the Spring of 1881, began to publish in Raton a paper called "The Comet," avowedly an anti-grant journal, which published fiery editorials on the Grant situation and incidentally took cracks at the liquor trade, but was practical enough, nevertheless, to run an advertisement of the "Little Buttercup" saloon in Raton. Not relying on the power of his pen entirely, McMains conducted anti-grant meetings, which assumed the fervor of old time revival gatherings. On August 19, 1882, McMains held an anti-grant meeting at McAuliffe & Ferguson's Hall, which was packed to the doors.

The Las Vegas Gazette of May 28, 1884, published a special dispatch from Raton, on the Grant situation, which among other things said:

> "Republicanism and democracy are all bosh and nonsense in the present condition of affairs in Colfax County, and never will the settlers here rally around their old time party ensigns until the Maxwell Land Grant is demolished, and this beautiful country is opened up for settlement by the sovereign people.
>
> "The only successful party that can exist here under these circumstances is the unqualified anti-grant, anti-land stealing and home robbing party, and the man or newspaper that advocates any other party or any other doctrine is no friend of the settlers and ought to be treated as such.
>
> "The ultimate success of the good work commenced by O. P. McMains can only be obtained by ignoring party lines and the good men of all parties uniting in striking a blow at the rings and monopolies that have been the curse of New Mexico for years, and at the same time annihilate politically those land sharks and ring masters and their confederates who like vampires have been preying and feeding upon the vitals of this county time out of mind."

Smart lawyers advised the anti-grant men to go into politics, to get themselves elected to local offices, levy heavy taxes, vote to issue bonds, build county roads, courthouses and improvements, which would give employment to large numbers of laboring men, all with a view to discouraging the Grant owners through imposition of heavy taxes. The anti-grant men were advised to favor "a large levy and rigid collection of taxes." The anti-grant lawyers said the Grant land was good "for Dutch guilders and English pounds."

The Maxwell Land Grant troubles finally assumed such proportions and became so important, that the United States government became interested, through litigation instituted in Colorado, but which applied to identical conditions with reference to the Grant in New Mexico.

During forty years subsequent to the American Occupation in 1846, the federal government had dealt in a slipshod manner with the Maxwell Land Grant. Opportunity after opportunity had presented itself to Washington either to acquire the Grant by purchase for the Indians or to do something constructive, by a thorough and careful survey by disinterested surveyors, and by a determination of the real meaning and intent of the description submitted by Miranda and Beaubien, granted by Governor Armijo in 1841; and through warding off the efforts of those who had been interested and instrumental in moving the title to the Grant, step by step, through federal and territorial legal facilities to ultimate legal security. But the federal authorities were not aggressively active in the matter while questions pertaining to confirmation and validation were in administrative and congressional procedure stages, where political manipulation, as it was freely charged by the anti-grant leaders, helped to make all things possible. Because New Mexico was a territory governed by remote control from Washington, the federal government was really the only authority involved, and Washington did not stir itself to action until, as the Supreme Court of the United States in effect held, the Grant matter was already "res adjudicata," a thing adjudged.

The United States of America, however, finally, belatedly,

got into action in the courts in connection with the affairs of the Maxwell Land Grant. A bill in equity was filed in the United States District Court in Colorado on August 25, 1882, some three years after the patent had been issued, against the Maxwell Land Grant Company, alleging also that John T. Elkins, Robert G. Marmon, Stephen B. Elkins, Harry Whigham and Frank Springer were all in possession of lands involved in the litigation, but were not made parties to the suit because they were non-residents of Colorado and not within the jurisdiction of the court.

The bill alleged that John T. Elkins and Robert G. Marmon, the surveyors of the Grant, "falsely, fraudulently and deceitfully," surveyed the land so as to take in and include a large number of acres of land not included in the original Grant. Paragraph 10 of the bill alleged that the Maxwell Land Grant & Railway Company, in the year 1877, officered by Stephen B. Elkins, president, together with Harry Whigham, secretary and treasurer, and Frank Springer, attorney for said company, "conspired with John T. Elkins, a brother of Stephen B. Elkins, and with Robert G. Marmon, surveyors of the Grant, to cheat and defraud the United States out of land by running an incorrect line, the land involved being in Las Animas County, Colorado, and containing 265,000 acres valued at $3,000,000.00."

Frank Springer entered his appearance in the cause, both in person and as attorney for the company, and participated actively in the litigation in the federal district court, and later in the Supreme Court of the United States. Lawyerlike pleadings were filed from time to time. The government, before actual trial began, softened somewhat in its allegations with reference to fraud and deceit, but still maintained that the survey lines had been incorrectly run and that the government was entitled to restitution of the land. Similar litigation was instituted in the courts in New Mexico, with an agreement that the parties would abide by the decision in the Colorado case. The testimony taken in the

Colorado litigation was most voluminous. The most important issue, of course, was the question of the correctness of the lines surveyed by Marmon and Elkins. The selection of John T. Elkins, a brother of Stephen B. Elkins, as one of the surveyors of the land grant, was indeed a most unfortunate and unhappy one. Stephen B. Elkins had been very active in negotiations for the financing of the enterprises and projects on the Grant, was president of the corporation which acquired the Grant from Lucien B. Maxwell, and had signed the bond for Marmon and John T. Elkins to guarantee the performance of their survey contract.

The contract for the survey was between Henry M. Atkinson, Surveyor-General of New Mexico, for and on behalf of the United States of America, and John T. Elkins and Robert G. Marmon, and was dated August 15, 1877. The contract price was $9,500 for a complete survey and the bond of $20,000 to guarantee the completion of the contract was signed by Stephen B. Elkins and James L. Johnson, as sureties. Days and days were consumed in taking testimony in regard to survey notes, natural monuments, boundaries, rivers, mountains, hills and valleys. Lucien B. Maxwell had been dead for several years at the time of the trial and the fact that his testimony was not available was an obstacle for the defenders in the litigation. The litigation, most of it highly technical in nature, threatened at times to become somewhat of an old timers' reunion. A number of pioneers gave their testimony to support the contention of one side to the litigation or the other, in regard to places, rivers and streams, tops of mountains.

Calvin Jones, one of the earliest mountain men in the country, testified on September 13, 1883, at which time he was sixty-one years old, that he had first gone into the Rayado with Kit Carson, "when there was plenty of deer and antelope," in the region.

When Calvin Jones began to testify about natural monu-

LUCIEN B. MAXWELL HOME AT FORT SUMNER

ments, place names and the early history of the country in question, the court and lawyers did not interrupt his reminiscences.

Calvin Jones said that in the fifties and sixties he had a large acquaintance with the Indian tribes of the region and talked some Cheyenne, Comanche and Arapahoe. He had wintered with them for several winters, trading for their furs. Telling about the names given to points of land, streams, or hills and mountains, in the region, and pointing to a map, Jones testified:

> "That Chicarica mesa—in former years there was a great quantity of birds, spotted, blue and white, upon it; something similar to the wild pigeon. The Comanches gave the name to the creek, 'Choco Rico.' The 'choco' is spotted and 'rico' is bird. They were birds that lived in the pine timber. That stream, Una de Gato, takes its name from a little bush, called, by the Americans, the black locust. From the thorns upon it, it takes its name. 'Una de Gato' is a cat's claw, and the thorns look like that. That Eagles Nest takes its name from the eagles building in the rocks and trees. Crow's Creek took its name in an early day, from a vast quantity of these birds that flew over this country, until they had to poison them. They built nests in the cottonwoods on the streams. This Raton Mountain takes its name from the gray squirrel, with a bushy tail and long ears, and the Mexicans called it 'raton.' The Chacuaco takes its name from a bush that grows in the canons. We called it the elder bush. The Mexicans called it 'chacuaco.' That is where the stream takes its name—from that bush. It grows there from a foot to a foot and a half through. San Francisco Mesa gets its name because one day there was a man by the name of Truhillo herding sheep down

there and this herder ran his sheep into a stream and drowned 800 or 900, and it took its name from the drowning of the sheep, Ahogadera; it is now called San Francisco mesa. When it was settled, the people who settled it did not like the name of the stream, and they met one day and appointed Judge Bransford to name the stream, and he called it San Francisco, and it has borne that name ever since.

"Manco de Burro Pass got its name first from a burro getting crippled, and the stream, also I understand, from the old settlers, that there was a pack train going through to trade with the Indians. Up on the mountains the burro put his knee out of place and limped and when anything limps, they say it is 'manco.' I heard of the Raton mesa before I came to this country. But the Ahogadera was not known by that until the country was settled up. The Ahogadera took its name in 1849 or 1850.

"I came first in 1848, but until 1849 or 1850 nobody ventured over this country. In the early days I did considerable trading with the Indians and met herdsmen and hunters also. There were many deer and antelope. I traded with the Cheyenne, Comanche and Arapahoes for furs, and spent several winters with them. Altogether I have spent thirty-nine years in the mountains and on the plains. I now reside in Las Animas County, about 30 miles east of Trinidad and am sixty-one years old the sixth day of March. I first became acquainted with Lucien B. Maxwell in the spring of 1848 when I went to the Rayado. I had left Bent's fort on the Arkansas in March with a herd of cattle to deliver to Lucien B. Maxwell. When I got to the Rayado, Maxwell was building a log house of three or four rooms. There was a man with him named Manuel La Favre, a carpenter, another man, whose name I have forgotten, and another man by the name of James White, also a carpenter. I was told by Maxwell that he had come over to the Rayado in February, across the mountains from Taos, with a little train of pack mules, and that he had been detained in the snow for some time, and lost a mule. I was employed by him for a time in 1848, then ran a train of oxen for a man named Joe Doyle, then traded with the Indians for some years and finally went back to Maxwell and worked for him two years and a half. I had charge of his sheep. He had 15,000 to 40,000 head of sheep. At different times he would sell off, lay in, lose and they generally ran on an average of 25,000 at a time. I worked for him two and a half years this time and quit in 1866."

Calvin Jones, questioned by the government, testified that in 1846, 1847 and 1848, the country east of the main range of the Rocky Mountains, in the northern part of New Mexico and southern portion of Colorado, was occupied by Indians, wild horses and buffalo, and that the only place on the Miranda and Beaubien Grant in those years occupied by civilized people was at Rayado, where there was one cabin and herders and cattle.

Among the important witnesses for the Maxwell Land Grant Company in the trial of the case in the Federal Court in Colorado, was "Uncle Dick" Wootton, already famous at the time he testified, in 1883, more famous with the passing of the years. Richens Lacy Wootton, a striking, picturesque character at the time of the litigation, was only sixty-seven years old, in good health and evidently possessing a fine memory for details. Wootton testified freely, and without much questioning by counsel. He told in considerable detail of his background and opportunities that had been afforded him to know the boundaries of the Maxwell Land Grant. "Uncle Dick" casually mentioned in the course of his testimony that he had been engaged at one time in smuggling goods into Mexico from the United States. That he had lived for many years a life of romance and adventure was evident throughout his testimony.

The former Virginian, many years a New Mexican, testified that he was born in Mecklenburg County, Virginia, in 1816; that he lived in the Raton Mountains about a mile and a half the other side of the tunnel; that since 1865 he had been keeping a toll road in the Raton Mountains. That he was known around the country as Dick Wootton and Uncle Dick—that he had been called Uncle Dick since 1859. That he came to the Rocky Mountain country in 1836, first arriving at Bent's old fort, about seven miles below La Junta, Colorado, on the north side of the Arkansas; that the fort was owned by Charles Bent and his brothers, William, George and Robert, and that Colonel St. Vrain was also interested in it.

"After my arrival at Bent's old fort," reminisced Uncle Dick, "I stayed there some twenty or thirty days; then there was a party of us went with some ox teams and some goods to the South Fork of the Platte, forty miles below where Denver now is, and from there we went across by Fort Laramie to a stream emptying into the North Fork of the Platte, called Rawhide; there we traded with a band of Sioux Indians, and then we returned from there, the same way we went, to Fort St. Vrain, on the South Fork of the Platte. We stayed there about twenty days, and then started out for Bent's fort on the Arkansas; there a party started out for Taos, under Col. St. Vrain, about eighteen or nineteen men in the party; we went within about twenty-six or seven miles of Taos.

"During the next few years I would trap and hunt in

the Spring and Fall in the mountains; during a number of years I was engaged in taking goods into Mexico to Beaubien. In 1841 I took a lot of sheep to Kansas City for a man named Kinkaid. In 1843 and 1844 I was engaged in catching buffalo calves and raising them in the summer time and in the winter time I was engaged in taking goods into New Mexico. I might really say, smuggling them in. Before 1848 the line between the United States and Mexico was the Arkansas River. In 1846, I was at Sierra Grande, trading with the Ute Indians, in the eastern part of what is now Colfax County, New Mexico. The next Spring, after the rebellion in Taos, I went into Taos to get some mules that had been taken away from me. Then I went into business at Taos, as a sutler for the First Dragoons and as a government contractor.
"I lived in Taos and made it my home until 1854. Then I moved down to the Arkansas River, where Huerfano empties into it, and established a trading post there. I remained there until the fall of 1856, when I moved down to the junction of the Sapello and Mora, in New Mexico, where Barclay's old fort was; and I stayed there until 1858. I then moved to where Denver now is; I remained there, I think, until the Fall of 1861, and then I moved down to within about nine miles of Pueblo and opened a ranch on the Fountain Quibouille. I remained there until 1864 and I moved to where Pueblo now stands and in 1865 moved to where I now live in the Raton Mountains. There I opened a toll road and have continued in the same business and have lived in the same place ever since. At different times I have while running the toll road, gone hunting and trapping and scouting through this region and sometimes I have been away as much

as three months at a time. I got acquainted with Kit Carson the first time in the Fall of 1837, I think it was in October. I was in his company a great deal at different times up to the time of his death. I was also well acquainted with Carlos Beaubien and with Cornelio Vigil. I also knew Jesus Silva, who worked for Judge Beaubien and later was a hunter and guide for the troops and finally worked for Lucien B. Maxwell. The first settlement on the Las Animas was in the Spring of 1846, when a man by the name of Hatcher built a cabin there about five or six miles from where El Moro now stands. The Indians run Hatcher off. In December 1858 I passed down the Las Animas, from where Trinidad now stands, to where El Moro is, and I didn't see a person or a house on that river. The first house that I saw after leaving Maxwell's on the Cimarron, going towards Denver, was on the Greenhorn, about seventy-five miles above Trinidad —north of Trinidad."

Getting down to the matter at hand, and away from his reminiscences, Uncle Dick Wootton testified that in February or March of 1843 he had run across a party composed of Carlos Beaubien, Jose Maria Valdez, Cornelio Vigil, Joaquin Le Roux, Jesus Silva and Pedro Miranda, a brother of Guadalupe Miranda, erecting a monument on Chicorica mesa, and that members of the party told him they were making a boundary of the Miranda-Beaubien Grant. "I knew the place," Wootton testified, "I had trapped on that stream, Chicorica. A trapper by the name of Bill Williams, who come to the country in 1831, was the man who took me there first. I went with him and a half-breed Indian named Amos."

Uncle Dick testified that some years before the railroad had come through, he had taken John Elkins and Marmon, surveyors, to the place where the mound had been erected, on the north edge of the northwest edge of the Chicorica mesa, and that Jesus Silva, Lucien B. Maxwell's old head man, had been with him, and they both showed the mound to the surveyors, which was in the same place that it had been in 1843. In attempting to fix the time when he had met the Alcade's party, going to set up the monument, Uncle Dick Wootton recalled that in December in 1842 he had made a trip into Taos, taking some goods in; that Col. St. Vrain was in Taos, and Charles Bent also.

> "A few days before Christmas, they started John Hawkins and myself out with ten pack animals loaded with silver, said to be sixty thousand dollars. I didn't count it. Hawkins and myself started about eleven or twelve o'clock in the night and they promised to send some men to overtake us. We also had about a thousand pounds of beaver skins. I got as far as the Trinchera west of Taos, and there I had to stop because I had no men. That was just about where Fort Garland is now. The snow was very deep and we had no men to pack the goods. They overtook me there with some men. This silver I was taking down to the old Fort Bent."

Uncle Dick Wootton volunteered the information that Lucien B. Maxwell had deeded him about 2500 acres of land in 1867, on part of which he had built his home. In return for the land Wootton had given Maxwell a perpetual right to pass over his toll road.

Harry Whigham, Assistant Secretary of the Maxwell Land Grant Company, testified during the trial that he was secretary of the Maxwell Land Grant and Railway Co., for a number of years; that the condition of the latter company beginning in 1875 and thereafter was that it was bankrupt; that all its personal property had been sold by the Sheriff to satisfy creditors; that his own salary was not paid for a long time; that the company's land was sold by the Sheriff for unpaid taxes; that the last president of the company had been Stephen B. Elkins in 1875; that the last directors were Stephen B. Elkins, Thomas B. Catron, R. H. Longwill, H. M. Porter and W. R. Morley; that W. T. Thornton had been appointed Receiver in 1878.

Frank Springer, undoubtedly the most gifted and brilliant man in the Maxwell Land Grant group, made a spirited defense of his position in the litigation, testifying that he was solicitor for the Maxwell Land Grant Company; that he had been counsel at various times for the Maxwell Land Grant and Railway Company from 1873 down to 1880. Springer said in his own defense:

> "I was upon unfriendly terms, personally and in business relations with Stephen B. Elkins, who had been formerly president and general counsel of the Maxwell Land Grant and Railway Company, and I considered the appointment of John T. Elkins to survey the boundaries of the Grant as antagonistic to the interests of the company I represented, because I understood that John T. Elkins, a brother of Stephen B. Elkins, had a contract to survey another grant, in which Stephen B. Elkins had an interest. I make this statement because in the bill of complaint originally filed in this cause and signed by the Attorney-General of the United States, I have been personally charged with conspiracy with Stephen B. Elkins and Marmon to defraud the government by inducing them to make a false survey; a charge which I here declare to be false in fact and based on no foundation and a wholly unwarranted attack upon the character of a private citizen. I now invite the fullest cross examina-

tion, not only upon the facts that I have stated but as to every other matter involved in this suit, and I waive every privilege of cross-examination."

Frank W. Springer was not cross-examined to any extent, and the case veered off into the financial phases of the project.

The District Court of the United States for the District of Colorado decided rather promptly that the government had not made out a very strong case against the Maxwell Land Grant Company and decided the case in favor of the Company, exonerating the corporation and its officers and all of the defendants in the cause from any taint of fraud, misconduct, deliberate mistakes in the survey or any other wrongdoing. The court said in United States v. Maxwell Land Grant Co., 26 Fed. 118:

> "I leave the case with the final observation, that after the fullest inquiry and observation by the government, with all the means and facilities at its command, the officials of the government and the claimants of the grant stand without a stain upon the rectitude of their conduct, and the boundaries of the grant, as finally surveyed and patented, if not proved to be absolutely accurate and correct, are at least shown to be as nearly so as any known testimony can determine."

The government took an appeal to the Supreme Court of the United States from Judge Brewer's decision.

CHAPTER X
The Vigilantes

GRANT and anti-grant troubles in Colfax County blazed high in the year 1885, centering in Raton. Under the leadership of Rev. O. P. McMains, publisher of the Raton Comet, the anti-grant men became more and more agitated. The Grant people had induced James H. Masterson, a brother of "Bat" Masterson, once town marshal of Dodge City, Kansas, to come to Raton, and had prevailed upon Governor Lionel A. Sheldon to quietly authorize the organization of a company of National Guards. The Raton Comet noted in its edition of February 27, 1885, that "last week two cases of arms addressed to James H. Masterson, Captain Company H, Territorial Militia, arrived at the express office in Raton." The Comet commented: "that this was the first news that Raton had that Governor Sheldon had organized a company of militia in Raton." The militia was to be formed with three commissioned officers, five non-commissioned officers and thirty-five privates. McMains published a letter in his paper on the same date from J. Osfield, Jr., referring to Rev. Mr. McMains as the man "who is opposed to this beautiful country of millions of acres being stolen by the vampires and land grant pirates of New Mexico."

The arrival of the arms in Raton, the knowledge, now public property, that Jim Masterson was to head a company of militia, that he was to select his own men, and that they were to be "killers," aroused the anti-grant men to a high pitch of excitement. A committee of Raton citizens left Raton at once by train for Santa Fe and interviewed Governor Sheldon, who gave them the information that he had been advised that soldiers would be required to enforce the decrees of the court in the ejectment suits of the Maxwell Land Grant Company, and it was on this supposition that he had authorized the organization of the militia company. Governor Sheldon, always called a "carpetbagger" by his enemies, promptly rescinded his orders, demanded that the militia company be disbanded. Company "H" was disbanded on March 1, 1885. In Raton, Jim Masterson resented the turn of events and during an argument pulled a gun on J. E. Herndon, whose name had been signed to a petition addressed to the Governor asking that the militia be disbanded. Masterson and some of his men went to Springer, the county seat, talking fighting words and making threats. Masterson and his "militiamen," it was claimed, were all "gunmen, killers, thugs and bums from places outside of New Mexico."

There was no room in Colfax County for a neutral. A man was either for or against the Grant. The Maxwell Land Grant Company was accused by the anti-grant men of having imported Jim Masterson and his crowd, and of having misled Governor Sheldon to the extent that he had clothed Masterson with power of the military branch of the government, with the right to use his fighters as a company of militia, with arms and ammunition furnished by the territory, to evict people from their claims on the Grant. George Curry, then a young man, later in 1908 Governor of the Territory of New Mexico, was in Raton in 1885, having recently returned from Lincoln County. As a boy George Curry had lived in Dodge City, Kansas, and knew both Bat Masterson and Jim Masterson. In Raton, Curry was employed by D. W. Stevens, a merchant who had befriended him on several occasions. While walking down the principal business street of Raton on the evening of March 9, 1885, Jim Masterson, without provocation, attacked Mr. Stevens, struck him on the head with a six-shooter and kicked him into the gutter. George Curry heard of the attack and immediately called a mass meeting, demonstrating to the public for the first time his amazing ability as an organizer, which won national fame and honor for him in later years.*

Leadership displayed by George Curry in organizing the Vigilantes and marking out a peaceful program for them in connection with the Jim Masterson militia incident marked the first step in a career which brought him fame in later years and the friendship of many noted men. Curry had seen life in the raw in Louisiana just after the Civil War. As a boy in Dodge City, Kansas, he had seen the toughest of the tough; consequently, "bad men" in New Mexico were no novelty to George Curry.

Essentially all his life a man of action, Curry became Governor of New Mexico twenty-two years after he had been jailed in Springer for rioting. In the intervening years he had gained fame as a captain in the United States army in Cuba, where he attracted the admiration of Colonel Theodore Roosevelt. After he became President of the United States, Roosevelt gave Curry a wide choice of places high in government service. Curry accepted a place as captain in the regular army in the Philippine Islands. William Howard Taft was governor-general of the Philippines. George Curry was made chief of police in Manila and given a free hand. He accomplished much in cleaning up the city. At times Governor-General Taft suggested that Curry pursue different methods in handling affairs in Manila. Curry's stock answer was always the same: "General, I am afraid the Colonel wouldn't like it that way." Once Taft cabled Roosevelt that a controversy existed between him and Curry over the

---

*George Curry was born in Bayou Sara, Louisiana, April 3, 1862. His father was George Curry, born in Kentucky; his mother was Clara Modden Curry, a native of Ireland. George Curry, Sr., was a soldier in the Confederate Army during the Civil War, was killed in 1872 as an outgrowth of his activities as an organizer of the Klu Klux Klan. Mrs. Clara Modden Curry moved with her four children to Dodge City, Kansas, in 1874. George Curry in childhood spent six months in school, never again entered a schoolroom until he was elected a school director in Lincoln County, New Mexico, in the Seventies, when he visited a school at Lincoln. Curry's mother died in Dodge City in 1877 and he and his brother John came to New Mexico. George Curry drifted from Raton to Lincoln County, where he was employed by James J. Dolan & Company, became assessor in 1890, sheriff in 1892, became president of the Thirty-first Territorial Council in 1893, Territorial Governor of New Mexico in 1907.

method of handling a problem. President Roosevelt's reply was terse, Rooseveltian: "Curry's wish is my command."

Before calling the mass meeting in Raton, Curry obtained from his employer a substantial sum of money, which he used to buy up every shotgun, pistol, rifle and every cartridge and shell in stock in every hardware store in Raton.

The indignation meeting was stealthily advertised by word of mouth. Under George Curry's direction, messengers were sent on horseback to Cow Creek and to the Vermejo and other places in the area. By eleven o'clock that night enough of the leaders from the Grant country were present to outline a course of action. It was decided to arrest Jim Masterson and every one of his militiamen and hold them in custody until the next day. George Curry personally obliged Jim Masterson to surrender to him in the Moulton Hotel in Raton. The meeting was held on March 10, 1885, in the Raton Rink, attended by 600 citizens. The program was businesslike. The meeting of the Raton Vigilantes was called to order by J. Osfield. H. A. McMartin was elected chairman, I. C. Showalter, secretary, T. P. Gable, George W. Geer, Thos. Ainsworth, D. W. Stevens and R. P. Lelton, vice-presidents. On motion of Rev. O. P. McMains, a committee was appointed to close all saloons in Raton. The committee immediately proceeded to close every saloon in Raton for the first time since the coming of the railroad. A committee of fifteen was appointed to escort Jim Masterson and the "other gentlemen to the Colorado line and enjoin upon them never to return." The Vigilantes elected Dick Rogers, a fearless cowboy, as captain, and Charles F. Hunt, later to become sheriff of Bernalillo County, New Mexico, as lieutenant. A member of the escorting committee was Thomas P. Gable, later Collector of Customs at the port of El Paso, Texas.

Due to the foresight of George Curry, there was no slip-up in the arrangements. One hundred fifty armed men patrolled the streets of Raton. No man suspected of being a "Masterson man" was permitted to retain his liberty. When the Vigilante mass meeting adjourned, the Masterson prisoners were given their noon-day meal, a procession was formed with 300 Vigilantes in line, and "the militiamen" were escorted to the Colorado line, given a lecture on what to do after they got there, were warned never to return to New Mexico, and "to live as honest men in the future."

Excitement had scarcely died down in connection with organization of the Jim Masterson company of militia, its disbandment by Governor Sheldon, and the Vigilante movement in Raton, when trouble broke out in Springer, the county seat of Colfax County. John Dodds and Sam Littrell, cowboys from a Cow Creek ranch, had gone to Springer on March 15, 1885, for a load of corn. John Dodds and Jesse Lee, a deputy sheriff in Springer, met on the street and renewed an old quarrel, an outgrowth of the militia company trouble. Lee had been a member of the company, but had not been in Raton on the day of the exodus. He was a gunman, and it was claimed, had been brought into Colfax County from Indian Territory by the Maxwell Land Grant Company. No one, however, had ever accused Jesse Lee of not being a crack shot and a cool, calculating man in an emergency. John Dodds got drunk in Springer, after his brush with Lee earlier in the day, and started to shoot up the town. He picked a quarrel in a saloon with Constable Carter, and bragged on the streets that he had whipped him in a fair fist fight. A warrant was sworn out for John Dodds, charging him with disturbing the peace. He was arrested, arraigned before Justice of the Peace Small in Springer, pleaded guilty, and paid a fine.

Believing that he had had enough excitement for one day, Cowboy Dodds started for home with his load of corn, but was overtaken by Deputy Sheriff Jesse Lee and Constable Carter a mile out of town, where they attempted to arrest him on a charge of assault made in a complaint signed by Carter. John

Dodds refused to submit to arrest and stood the officers back with his six-shooter. When Lee and Carter had given up trying to arrest him, John Dodds returned to Springer and telegraphed Dick Rogers, captain of the Vigilantes at Raton. Rogers started for Springer and was joined at Cow Creek enroute by "Red River" Tom Whealington, John Curry, a brother of George Curry, and Bob Lee. By the time Dick Rogers had arrived in Springer, the anti-grant war was on again. Cowboys and anti-grant men gathered from every trail, ranchhouse and settlement. In the meantime, Jesse Lee had arrested Cowboy John Dodds and put him in the county jail at Springer. Word went out that Dodds was to be delivered from jail by the mob, with Dick Rogers, captain of the Vigilantes, in command. Jack Williams, United States Deputy Marshal, had an idea, however, that he could arrange terms with Jesse Lee, and shouted out to the crowd, "One of you come with me! Everybody keep quiet. I will go to the jail. Jesse Lee knows me."

Dick Rogers and Jack Williams, both unarmed and on a mission of peace, as it was later claimed, approached the county jail. As they neared the building, Jesse Lee, Deputy Kimberly and Deputy Duce Hixenbaugh opened fire, killing Dick Rogers, leader of the Vigilantes. "Red River" Tom Whealington galloped up on his horse, jumped off and picked up the body of Rogers. John Curry rushed toward the jail on foot, Winchester in hand. Jesse Lee shot John Curry, mortally wounding him, and a moment later shot and killed "Red River" Tom Whealington. When a Vigilante went to his aid, John Curry said he was all right, except that he seemed to be paralyzed in the back, and asked to have his hat placed under his head for a pillow. John Howe, Bob Lee and George Curry rushed to the jail and emptied their guns at the crowd in the courthouse. George Curry then went for a wagon in which to carry away the bodies of Dick Rogers and Tom Whealington, and to get medical assistance for his brother John. John Curry, who had been shot in the spine and paralyzed from the waist down, died at two o'clock the next morning in the arms of his brother, George Curry, at the Springer Hotel. A mere boy, nineteen years old when he died, John Curry's mind was clear to the end and he made no complaint, although suffering greatly.

George Curry in the meantime had telegraphed to Raton for help and a crowd of forty men left there at once for Springer, having elected John McKown and Charles F. Hunt as commanders of the party. Arriving in Springer they viewed the bodies of Dick Rogers, Tom Whealington and John Curry.

District Attorney Melvin W. Mills, sensing that the Vigilantes would renew the fight and kill "the courthouse crowd," found that the Vigilantes had taken charge of the Santa Fe Railway Station at Springer, had posted an armed guard at the telegraph key, and notified the telegraph operator that he would be killed instantly if he disobeyed orders. Mills left Springer for Wagon Mound by team as soon as the shooting had subsided, and from there telegraphed Acting Governor Losch for aid. Acting Governor Losch telegraphed General Bradley, Commander of the Department of New Mexico, who ordered two officers of the United States army at Fort Union to proceed with twenty men to Watrous, where a special train took them to Springer. The detachment of soldiers was in charge of Captain Joel Kirkman of the U. S. 10th Infantry.

The Vigilantes refused to allow the soldiers to go to the courthouse and jail. Captain Kirkman finally asked the Vigilantes to name a committee to confer with the officers. The Vigilantes named Marion Littrell, later sheriff of Colfax County for many years, Charles F. Hunt, Thomas P. Gable and George Curry, to attend the conference. As a result of the conference Jesse Lee was placed under arrest by the soldiers and taken to Las Vegas for safekeeping, accompanied by a Vigilante committee composed of Marion Littrell, George Curry, Ed. King, James Smith, Ira Gale and Will South. Jesse Lee obtained a change of venue from Colfax County to Taos County, but he was never tried.

Judge Samuel B. Axtell, Chief Justice of the Territory, issued a bench warrant for George Curry and had him put in jail in Springer. After being in jail for three weeks, Curry finally made bond in the sum of $5,000. Thomas Benton Catron of Santa Fe was employed by the land grant crowd as special counsel to prosecute Curry. The Vigilantes were anxious to murder Tom Catron, not only for accepting the work of special prosecutor, but for the work he had done in civil cases in ejecting settlers from the Maxwell Land Grant. George Curry counselled peace and patience and prevented harm to Catron. For several years after the fight, Thomas Benton Catron remained away from Springer and Cimarron. He had been warned by the Vigilantes that his life would pay for a visit to that country.

Funeral services for Dick Rogers, 28, from Texas, Tom Whealington, 28, from Texas, and John Curry, 19, from Louisiana, by way of Dodge City, were held in Raton on St. Patrick's Day, March 17, 1885. The entire countryside turned out for the services. All saloons were closed. There was no work at the mines at Blossburg, or the railway shops at Raton. The Vigilantes attended in great numbers. Three ministers of the gospel officiated, Rev. J. W. Sinnock, Rev. J. McGaughey and Rev. E. Burch.

Dick Rogers, one of the men killed at Springer, had been in Lincoln County War several years before moving to Colfax County, claiming to have fought on the side of "law and order." He was also credited with having saved the life of Jesse Lee in Raton two weeks before Lee shot and killed him.

The killing of Dick Rogers, Tom Whealington and John Curry marked a high point in the resistance of the anti-grant people to what was described as constituted authority. With ejectment suits and court injunctions being available to the owners of the Grant, the settlers one by one began to bow to the inevitable. The Vigilantes began to disband.

The settlers, who had expected to ultimately have their titles quieted, either left the country or made their peace with the owners of the property. The Gringo had found out, as the Utes and Jicarilla Apaches had discovered and as the Spanish-American settlers were beginning to find out, that they only thought they had rights on the Grant.

CHAPTER XI
The Supreme Court

THE United States District Court for the District of Colorado having rendered a decision adverse to the contentions of the federal government, an appeal was perfected in the Supreme Court of the United States. The record in the case on appeal was impressive. The transcript of testimony, exhibits, briefs and other pleadings made up a total of some nine hundred printed pages. The case was argued before the Supreme Court in Washington on March 8, 9, 10 and 11, 1887, four days having been devoted by the court to hearing the arguments of counsel, William A. Maury, Assistant Attorney-General of the United States, and J. A. Bentley, Special Assistant, for the government, and Frank W. Springer and Charles E. Gast for the Maxwell Land Grant Company.

The Supreme Court handed down an opinion five weeks after the oral arguments had been submitted.* On April 18, 1887, Mr. Justice Miller for the court delivered the opinion orally from the bench. Neither in the opinion of the Supreme Court of the United States, nor in the opinion of the Federal District Court of Colorado was particular reference made to the historical atmosphere or economic situation that had surrounded the Grant from the beginning. No mention whatever was made of the Indians, who still believed they owned the Grant, or of the many Spanish-American and American settlers who still were claiming rights on the Grant. Apparently adequate emphasis had never been placed in any of the litigation, either by court

*United States v. The Maxwell Land Grant Company, et al. 121 U. S. 325, 30 L. ed. 949.

or counsel, upon the purpose behind the policy of the Mexican government in making grants of land. No great point was ever made in the courts to the provisions of Article 12 of the decree of the Mexican Congress of 1824 in regard to land grants, that the grants were to be made to "empressarios, for them to colonize with many families."

The opinion of the Supreme Court of the United States was scholarly and elaborate, touching at considerable length upon many facts incident to the establishment of the Grant and the legal propositions involved. The court based its decision mainly on the fact that the Grant had been confirmed by Act of Congress, approved June 21, 1860, entitled, "An Act to Confirm Certain Private Land Claims in the Territory of New Mexico," 12 St. at L. 71, and declared that no power existed in the courts to annul an Act of Congress, citing Article 4, Section 1 of the Constitution of the United States, providing that, "The Congress shall have power to dispose of all needful rules and regulations respecting the territory, or other property, belonging to the United States."

Justice Miller, who wrote the opinion, declared that the Congress had passed upon and settled the question, and held that whatever rights which had not been vested in Miranda and Beaubien prior to confirmation, and which had been vested in the United States of America, had been conveyed to them by the Act of Congress in confirmation. Saying that it could not be easily perceived how the courts of the United States could set aside the action of Congress, the opinion went on to hold that the government had failed utterly to establish by any substantial evidence any acts of fraud or mistake in the surveys in connection with the Grant boundaries or otherwise.

The Supreme Court of the United States, by its decision, confirmed in Miranda and Beaubien and their grantees, the tract of land described in the patent previously issued by the government of the United States for 1,714,764.93 acres lying partly in New Mexico, partly in Colorado.

A petition for rehearing was filed in the Supreme Court of the United States, submitted on May 12, 1887, and promptly decided, the opinion on the rehearing being handed down on May 27, 1887.* Mr. Justice Miller again delivered the opinion of the court saying that, "on account of the importance of the matter involved, as well as the interest in it manifested by the Department of the Interior," the court had considered the petition very fully, and, departing from its custom, would make some response to its suggestions. The court stood by its original opinion, but evaded the claim of the government that it had in its possession new and material evidence touching the fundamental character of the Grant. The court complimented counsel, saying: "The case itself has been pending in the courts of the United States since August 1882, and on account of its importance, was advanced out of order for hearing in this court. The arguments on both sides of the case were unrestricted in point of time, and were wanting in no element of ability, industrious research, or clear apprehension of the principles involved in it."

The court, in its valedictory, said: "The result is that we are entirely satisfied that the Grant, as confirmed by the action of Congress, is a valid grant; that the survey and the patent issued upon it are entirely free from any fraud on the part of the grantees or those claiming under them; and that the decision could be no other than that which the learned judge of the circuit court below made, and which this court affirmed."

The decision of the highest court in the land on the Maxwell Land Grant case was a cause for great elation on the part of those financially or otherwise interested in the enterprise. The victory in the Supreme Court was especially gratifying to Frank

*United States v. The Maxwell Land Grant Company, et al, 122 U. S. 365, 30, L. ed. 1211.

W. Springer, of Cimarron, who had managed the litigation from the beginning and had personally tried and argued the case in the Federal District Court in Colorado as well as in the Supreme Court in Washington. Springer's zeal and learning, his outstanding ability as a lawyer, his great industry and perseverance had never been put to a greater test, or been more magnificently rewarded. Successful termination of the litigation was a great tribute to Frank W. Springer personally and marked the zenith of his career as a member of the bar in New Mexico.

In the hills and valleys of the immense country that made up the Maxwell Land Grant, when the news of the decision of the Supreme Court had become generally known, there prevailed great disappointment and an atmosphere of gloom and defeat. Many families over a great many years had settled on the Grant in entire good faith, believing that in time their claims would ripen into perfect title and that they would not be molested in their possession of the homesteads and ranches upon which they had made their homes. Now the people were apprehensive, fearful of the next move to be made by the Grant owners, sullen in their resentment.

CHAPTER XII
The Financial Aspects

ON MAY 6, 1869, for a consideration of twelve thousand dollars, Lucien B. Maxwell and Luz Beaubien Maxwell, his wife, entered into an agreement with Jerome B. Chaffee, George M. Chilcott and Charles F. Holly, giving them an option to purchase the Maxwell Land Grant for six hundred fifty thousand dollars, representing that it contained about 2,000,000 acres of land. Wilson Waddingham, a prominent land speculator of the time, and others, were associated with Chaffee in the transaction. On June 12, 1869, Maxwell was notified that Chaffee and associates had elected to exercise the option to purchase, and advised him that arrangements had been made to sell the property for $1,350,000, or more than double the amount specified in the option. When Chaffee, Waddingham and other promoters obtained the option on the Grant from Lucien B. Maxwell, they represented British capital. The promoters assigned their rights to the Maxwell Land Grant & Railway Company, a corporation created by an Act of the Legislature of New Mexico.

On April 30, 1870, the Maxwells conveyed the Grant for a consideration of one million three hundred fifty thousand dollars to the newly organized corporation. Revenue stamps in the amount of $1,350 were affixed to the deed. The Maxwells reserved in their conveyance a home ranch of about one thousand acres. On June 30, 1870, the property was mortgaged by the corporation for seven hundred thousand pounds sterling, or eight million four hundred thousand Dutch guilders, with interest at seven per cent., payable either in London or Amsterdam. On November 1, 1872, a second mortgage was placed against the property to secure a loan of two hundred seventy-five thousand pounds sterling, with the Farmers' Loan and Trust Company of New York named as the trustee. On March 11, 1878, both mortgages were foreclosed for the benefit of the bondholders and reorganization was effected May 3, 1880. The Maxwell Land Grant and Railway Company had been a stock and bond selling scheme. The promoters had made a fortune in the transaction. Even without the fight on the title, it is doubtful if the enterprise could have been successfully carried on. Money was spent lavishly in the promotion of the sale of the mortgage bonds on the Grant property. There never was much question, after the investigations had been made by bondholders, that the entire business had been poorly handled.

When the investing public in England and Holland had been called upon to buy mortgage bonds of the Maxwell Land Grant and Railway Company, the investors and their counsel required opinions on the title of the Grant and the validity of the bonds. These were obtained by the promoters from some of the best known lawyers of the day, men of national and international reputations.

The bond sellers submitted opinions of Noah Davis, dated July 20, 1870, of Wm. M. Evarts, dated July 20, 1870, of T. F. Bayard, dated July 21, 1870, of George T. Curtis, dated July 28, 1870, and finally, but not least important, the opinion of Judah P. Benjamin, then at the Temple Inn in London, dated January 18, 1871. Benjamin had been United States Senator from Louisiana before the Civil War, and a member of the cabinet of President Jefferson Davis, of the Confederate States of America during that war. All of these distinguished gentlemen of the bar, without dissent, concurred in the opinion that the Maxwell Grant, made by Governor Manuel Armijo, Governor of the Department of New Mexico, to Carlos Beaubien and

THE FINANCIAL ASPECTS 115

Guadalupe Miranda on January 11, 1841, confirmed by Act of Congress, by the Act of June 21, 1860, was a valid grant, that the title was perfect, indefeasible. The opinions of Davis, Evarts, Bayard, Curtis and Benjamin, all noted and brilliant members of the Bar of that day, gave evidence of serious study of the questions involved. Most of them reached their conclusions by the same routine of thought and consideration.

The opinion of Judah P. Benjamin was especially painstaking, and was significant because he had been chairman of the committee of the United States Senate which had passed upon and approved "Claim No. 15," which was the Maxwell Land Grant claim, and which preceded the enactment by the Congress of the United States of the Act of June 21, 1860, by which the United States of America confirmed the claim and quitclaimed all "right, title and interest of the United States therein," saving only the rights of adverse claimants, "if any there might be." It is important to recall that the Act of June 21, 1860, approved the claim and quitclaimed the interests of the federal government for an unknown quantity of land. The Act of Congress simply approved "Claim No. 15" along with a number of other claims, and rejected, or modified two or three other numbered claims. When Judah P. Benjamin was asked for an opinion on the Grant, he was no stranger to the procedure by which the Congress of the United States had given its blessing to the legality of the Grant. It is doubtful, however, if Benjamin, while in the United States Senate and serving as chairman of the Public Lands Committee, had ever given more than a passing thought to the Grant, or had even the most remote idea of the immense tract of land which the Congress was in effect conveying and confirming to the claimants.

The opinion of Judah P. Benjamin, dated some six months after the opinions of the other distinguished members of the bar was perhaps to fortify their opinion, although it is known that Benjamin in England early in 1870 had given an answer, to parties desiring to purchase the Grant, on one question—as to whether the Act of Congress of June 21, 1860, formed a valid title to the Grant against the United States. Benjamin's opinion then on the sole question asked was "that the said Act of Congress formed a valid title to the said Grant as against the United States." *** "I advised that the said Act constituted the highest title known to the law of the United States for said Claim No. 15," said Benjamin, "inasmuch as it emanated from the legislative and executive departments together (the law having been approved by the President), whereas a patent is issued by the Executive alone, and is void when made in contravention of law." (Opinion of Benjamin, January 18, 1871.)

Some seventeen years later the Supreme Court of the United States sustained the opinions that had been given by distinguished counsel, Davis, Evarts, Bayard, Curtis and Benjamin.

With the collapse of the Maxwell Land Grant and Railway Company, a new group of speculators took hold of the project. A new corporation was organized under the laws of Holland known as the Maxwell Land Grant Company. Frank R. Sherwin took the lead in the promotion of the reorganization of the affairs of the enterprise. The Grant property was sold to Sherwin at foreclosure sale for $2,000,000 on March 1, 1880. Sherwin had associated with him in America men of national reputation at the time, including N. K. Fairbank, George M. Pullman and George P. Carpenter. Commenting on the outlook for the enterprise under new financial control, the "Las Vegas Gazette" of March 25, 1880, said in an editorial:

> "This will certainly be a strong company. It is to be hoped that the disputes which have rendered this grant almost a dead sea at the very threshold of New Mexico are finally settled and that the grant will be separated into smaller parcels and sold out to settlers. It is a princely estate, embracing immense coal fields, vast forests of timber, rich placer and lode mines of

silver and gold, and fine pasture and agriculture land."

That the Elkins-Marmon survey had considerable to do with the determination of Sherwin and his associates to become interested in the affairs of the Grant was apparent from the testimony Sherwin gave at the time of the trial in the United States District Court in Colorado on the questions pertaining to the boundaries of the Grant. When the Maxwell Land Grant and Railway Company was wrecked financially, it was a real wreck, according to Sherwin. On this phase of the subject, Sherwin testified:

> "If you had been holding any of the company's paper at the time, 1875 or 1876, you would have thought it the most hopeless wreck you ever saw. The first mortgage bonds of the company were quoted at four or five cents on the dollar and were not salable at that. You could get one hundred thousand dollars of the floating debt for the price of a cigar."

A committee was organized, Sherwin said, in Amsterdam to represent bondholders and shareholders, but those financially interested refused to put any more money into the venture; the property had been sold a time or two for taxes; T. B. Catron had bought up the property at one tax sale. Sherwin testified that after he learned of the Elkins survey, he got active in dealing with bondholders' certificates, with the result that he helped reorganize the affairs of the company. He bought up large blocks of the paper of the company, interested capital in organizing the Maxwell Land Grant Company in the spring of 1880, elected a board of eight directors: F. H. Zielgelaar, F. A. Van Hall, Count Van Limburg-Stirum and A. A. De Sarlangre, all of Amsterdam, Holland, N. K. Fairbank, George M. Pullman and George P. Carpenter of Chicago, and himself, Sherwin. Sherwin was elected president. A. W. Anderson, the English Consul in Amsterdam, was appointed secretary of the new company, and Harry Whigham of Cimarron, assistant secretary.

During the period of reorganization of the Maxwell Land Grant and Railway Company, Sherwin assumed management of the financial end of the business in the old world. The stock was sold and resold many times. "I should think," Sherwin testified, "that in one hundred days the entire property changed hands a couple of times. The certificates representing the bonds advanced from about five cents on a dollar, where they stood just previous to my knowledge of the completion of the Elkins survey, to 55, and even touching sixty, just previous to the reorganization and formation of the new company. It was the leading speculative feature on the Amsterdam market . . . "

In summing up, in his brief, on an appeal to the Supreme Court of the United States, J. A. Bentley, special assistant U. S. Attorney, commenting on this phase of the business, said:

> "The case then is, the Maxwell Land Grant Railway Company, a corporation organized in New Mexico to purchase the Beaubien and Miranda Grant after the Secretary of the Interior had decided that its extent did not exceed 22 square leagues altogether, purchased the Grant, issued and sold its bonds, secured by a mortgage on the Grant, to purchasers bound to know the state of the title and extent of the Grant, and after default in the payment of the bonds, while the officers of the company manipulated affairs to enlarge the Grant, outside speculators bought up the bonds at a small percentage of their face, foreclosed the mortgage, bought in the property at foreclosure sale, organized themselves into a corporation in a foreign country, transferred their title to a new corporation, and then alleged against the government that the new corporation is a bona fide purchaser of the enlarged grant for value. The statement is a conclusive answer to the pretension."

CHAPTER XIII

Spanish Americans

THE Maxwell Land Grant Company, successor in title to the grant of the Maxwell Land Grant and Railway Company, well capitalized, fortified by the decision of the Supreme Court of the United States sustaining the title to the Grant, and with definite plans for the management of the property, adopted a firm policy in dealing with settlers on the Grant. Many suits were filed in the courts seeking the ejectment of the so-called squatters. The extraordinary remedy of injunction was resorted to by the Company in an effort to prohibit the settlers from remaining on land they believed they had homesteaded. Many settlers based their rights on the final action of the Commissioner of Public Lands of the United States in 1874 in throwing open to preemption settlement as public land the entire Maxwell Grant tract. See Mis. Doc. No. 201, 49th Congress, 1st Session; and House R. No. 1824, 52nd Congress, 1st Session. Other settlers who had been on the land for many years, although having no paper evidence of title, claimed title by adverse possession. Ejectment suit after ejectment suit was filed against the Whitefords, the Lynches, Newtons, Camerons and others. The court dockets of the period were filled with entries relating to the litigation involving the lands claimed by the settlers. A sample of the suits filed against the Spanish-American settlers on the Grant was that of Maxwell Land Grant Company, "a corporation created and organized under a charter from the King of the Netherlands, pursuant to the laws of the Kingdom of Netherlands, doing business within the Territory of

119

New Mexico," filed in the district court of Colfax County, New Mexico, on April 24, 1884. Defendants named in the suit, it was claimed, were wrongfully in occupation of lands "along the valley of the Cimarron River between the fence of what is known as the Johnson Ranch, now occupied by Henry Lambert, and the junction of the Cimarron and Rayado Rivers." It was alleged that the defendants were using the land "to herd and pasture large herds of sheep, cattle, goats and other animals," and were "cutting hay for miles in many directions, and fencing tracts of land for miles on both sides of the Cimarron."

The lawsuit was striking at men who, with their ancestors, had been on the Grant at San Andres settlement and vicinity before Lucien B. Maxwell had arrived in New Mexico. They had built their homes and their churches in settlements, established their way of life. Some of the defendants in this particular case, filed by Frank Springer and Thomas Benton Catron representing the company, were the following: Pablo Zamora, Emerjildo Zamora, Jesus Maria Arellano, Manuel Arellano, Juan Sandoval, Petrolino Padilla, Manuel Fernandez, Jose Gutierrez, Narcisco Martinez, Antonio Martinez, Juan Valdez, Juan Romero, Dolores Casias, Cristobal de Herrera, Francisco Perea, Miguel Gutierrez, Juan P. Herrera, Vicente Zamora, Bartolo Vigil, Anastacio de Herrera, Luis de Herrera, Pedro Sanchez, Romulo Sandoval, Andres Fernandez, Estefano Deacy, Anastacio Arellano, Domingo Sandoval, Miguel Herrera, Santos Padilla, Francisco Vialpando, Librado Zamora, Juan Cordoba, Mateo Cordova, Julian Lopez, Isabel Moreno, Ana Maria Solano, Iresano Padilla, Sisto Carillo, Rafael Lucero, Manuel Gonzales, Jose Zamora. These men, with their families, many of them from Taos and vicinity, had either ranches, farms or grazing lands on the Grant. The prophecy of Padre Martinez, who predicted that the people would be in difficulty over the Grant and its boundaries, had come true. Oldtimers recalled that the Curate of Taos had protested to Governor Armijo in an

George Curry

effort to save the rights of the people of Taos in connection with the Grant.

S. B. Axtell, Chief Justice of the Supreme Court of the Territory and Judge of the First District, on affidavit of Frank Springer, issued a temporary injunction requiring the defendants to show cause before the court on May 2, 1884. The temporary injunction was sweeping in character and prohibited even grazing of animals on the disputed territory "until the further order of the court." The defendants answered, setting up that they had been in possession of the lands many years before the Maxwell Land Grant Company had any existence, that "they resided upon and occupied their lands upon the Cimarron River and had cultivated the same, and cut grass therefrom for many years, had grazed their sheep, cattle and goats on the lands, which were open prairie extending many miles in every direction, as far back as the present inhabitants have any knowledge," and that "no person claiming such lands had ever forbidden the use and occupation of the same." The defendants further claimed that they were the owners of "separate and distinct parcels of land lying in the valley of the Cimarron River," and that the animals grazing on the prairie were not jointly, but separately owned.

The litigation for years dragged on its weary way and was finally referred to Charles M. Bayne, as special master, who heard testimony at Springer on April 29, 1887. The Maxwell Land Grant Company through its attorney, Frank Springer, submitted its legal title papers as evidence of right to possession. The report of the special master, Charles M. Bayne, a justice of the peace and fire insurance agent at Raton, was in favor of the company, against the people on the Cimarron. The report was adopted in full by the court, "ratified and confirmed." The company was declared to be the owner of all the lands involved and all of the defendants, "their officers, agents and servants" were perpetually prohibited by the court from "in any manner occupying, holding or possessing any lands within the limits" of the Maxwell Land Grant, or "from cutting, removing or appropriating to their own use" any grass or hay grown thereon, "or from herding or pasturing upon said lands or any part thereof any sheep, cattle, goats or other animals." Judge James O'Brien, the district judge who signed the decree at Springer on October 15, 1892, ordered the defendants to pay the court costs. There was much talk that the settlers had been "sold out," but nothing came of the talk.

Thus ended the efforts of one group of settlers of Spanish and Mexican descent to hold lands they claimed along the Cimarron River. Discouraged by the long drawn out litigation, the settlers found themselves without their homes or their pastures for grazing animals, disinherited and dislocated. These people, alien in 1846, who had become citizens of the United States under the terms of the Treaty of Guadalupe Hidalgo between the United States and Mexico in 1848, found themselves, after the decree of 1892, in pretty much the same condition in which the Utes and Jicarilla Apaches had found themselves some years before. The Indians had been deprived of their ancestral lands without benefit of a court order, but finally the federal government had, with some degree of enlightenment and intelligence, led them to reservations which had been set aside for them, gave them rations, undertook to educate them in the ways of the American. The settlers of Spanish and Mexican ancestors, more intelligent, and more capable of assimilating quickly the ways of the American, if opportunity had been afforded, had been left with their families and their animals to depend upon their own resources. No helping hand had been extended to them by the United States of America. Primarily a pastoral and agricultural people, possessing great ability and patience in those fields of useful endeavor, they looked elsewhere for grazing lands and home lands, and found but scant encouragement. In every direction there was the land grant, large tracts of land claimed by some smart Gringo speculator, posted against occupation or grazing. No wonder many of the men, driven by injunction and claim of superior title held by owners of the Maxwell Land Grant, losing their courage, dignity and initiative, moved back into settlements, sat down along adobe walls, and dreamed of other and better days.*

* The quarrel in 1844, under Mexican rule, between Padre Martinez, of Taos, and Carlos Beaubien and Guadalupe Miranda, over the Maxwell Land Grant and its boundaries was undoubtedly one of the most important contributing factors to the Taos Massacre of January 18, 1847. Representing his people in Taos, Martinez had claimed, but Beaubien and Miranda had denied, that Charles Bent was interested in the ownership of the Grant. Kearney and Doniphan took over New Mexico in 1846. Beaubien, the Canadian, who claimed in his petition for the grant, that he was a citizen of Mexico, demonstrated how uncertain had been his Mexican citizenship, by accepting appointment as a justice of the territorial supreme court after the American Occupation. Subsequent to 1846 no secret was made to Bent's claim to part ownership in the Grant. In the Taos massacre, when the Mexicans and Indians revolted, the plotters killed Governor Charles Bent, interested in the Grant, Narcisco Beaubien, a son of Carlos Beaubien, Cornelio Vigil, a Justice of the Peace in Taos under Mexican rule, and who had placed Beaubien and Miranda in possession of the Grant, and others who had been on Bent's side in the Grant fight in Taos.

CHAPTER XIV

Claims of Land Stealing

INDIVIDUALS claiming land on the Maxwell Land Grant found that it was impossible, without plenty of money, to litigate questions of law and of fact in the courts against able counsel employed by the Grant Company. The Vigilante affair at Raton and the riot at Springer, however, had served to focus attention, not only on the affairs of the Maxwell Land Grant but to bring national attention to the land grant problem generally in New Mexico. Maxwell Land Grant troubles, open and frequent charges of fraud and corruption, of descriptions that were "vastly expanded upon and enlarged," it was claimed, raised such a stink in New Mexico and in Washington that finally the Court of Private Land Claims was established in New Mexico.

The New Mexico land grant problem was brought to the attention of President Grover Cleveland as early as 1885. President Cleveland, under date of May 11, 1885, appointed George W. Julian as Surveyor-General of New Mexico. Julian, seventy years old at the time of his appointment, entered upon the duties of his office with the zeal of a crusader, on July 22, 1885. The newspaper editors of the day in New Mexico dubbed him "Old Malaria." The new surveyor-general claimed that President Cleveland had asked him to cooperate with him in breaking up the rings in the territory of New Mexico.

Arriving in Santa Fe, Julian asked no odds of any man. He discovered that when New Mexico had been ceded to the United States by Mexico, the estimated area of the land grants made under Spanish and Mexican rule was 24,000 square miles, or something over 15,000,000 acres, equal in extent to the land surface of four states in New England, Rhode Island, Connecticut, New Hampshire and Vermont; found that the Treaty of Guadalupe Hidalgo of 1848, and the Law of Nations, obliged the United States to protect the title to all of the grants, so far as found valid under the laws of Spain and Mexico; found that the Congress of the United States had passed the Act of July 22, 1854, creating the office of Surveyor-General of New Mexico, making it his duty to "ascertain the origin, nature, character and extent" of land grant claims, and to report his findings to the Congress for final action.

The Act of 1854 armed the surveyor-general with great power and responsibility. Julian, the new surveyor-general, complained that "the legislation by congress would have proved wise and salutary if the surveyor-generals had been first rate lawyers, incorruptible men, and diligent in their work, and if congess had promptly acted upon the cases reported for final decision." But, Julian contended, "the reverse of all this happened. Competent and fit men for so important a service would not accept the place for the meager salary provided by law. Official life in a former Mexican province, and in the midst of an alien race, offered few attractions to men of ambition and force. Moreover, the men who could be picked up for the work were exposed to very great trials. Their duties presupposed judicial training and an adequate knowledge of both Spanish and American law, but with one or two exceptions they were not lawyers at all, while they were clothed with the power to adjudicate the title to vast areas of land. Of course, the speculators who bought these grants at low rates from the grantees, or their descendants, comprehended the situation perfectly. They sought the good will of the Surveyor-General because they desired an opinion favorable to their titles. In furtherance of this daring purpose they took note of his small salary and natural love of thrift, while carefully taking his measure with the view of enlisting him in their service by controlling motives. It quite naturally happened that forged and fraudulent grants, covering very large tracts, were declared valid, and that the Surveyor-General's office very often became a mere bureau in the service of grant claimants, and not the agent and representative of the government.*

Surveyor-General Julian worked day and night in his new position. Not content with diligently attending to the duties of his office, Surveyor-General Julian raked the "grant ring," fore and aft, with verbal broadsides printed in such New Mexican newspapers and nationally known magazines as would print his articles and interviews. Julian wrote a series of articles for the North American Review in 1887,* in which he condemned the practices of surveyors-general who had preceded him in office, cited specific instances of what he termed fraudulent grants, and recommended finally that all land grant cases be referred to the Secretary of the Interior for final consideration. Congress, he contended, by "slipshod legislation in dealing with these grants, has surrendered to monopolists and thieves millions of acres of the public domain."

Critical of Congress, Julian said it would be "folly to lay all the blame on the Surveyors-General of New Mexico." The House Committee on Private Land Claims of the Thirty-sixth Congress, Julian claimed, in its report recommending the approval of fourteen claims, emphasized the incompetency of these surveyors-general for the adjudication of such cases. In commenting on the Maxwell Land Grant case,* Julian contended that grant had been "limited by the law under which it was made to twenty-two square leagues, or about 96,000 acres." But, Julian said, "it had been surveyed and patented for 1,714,764 acres, or nearly 2,680 square miles. This was done in 1879, in

*North American Review, Vol. 145. July to December, 1887, pp. 17-31
*Ibid
*Ibid

violation of an express order of the Secretary of the Interior, made ten years before, and still in force, restricting it to twenty-two square leagues, and the patent for the larger area issued under circumstances indicating the remarkable readiness of the Commissioner of the General Land Office and the Surveyor-General to serve the claimants."

"But this astounding piracy of the public domain did not originate with these officials," Julian continued. "It had an earlier genesis. Congress had been beguiled by the claimants in 1860 into the confirmation of the Grant, with the exterior boundaries named in it, which covered the whole of this immense area, and thus vested the title thereto in the grantees, as the Supreme Court of the United States has recently decided. Congress laid the egg in 1860, which was kindly incubated by the Commissioner of the General Land Office and the Secretary of the Interior in 1879. It was an inexcusable and shameful surrender to the rapacity of monopolists of 1,662,764 acres of public domain, on which hundreds of poor men had settled in good faith, and made valuable improvements, while it has been as calamitous to New Mexico as it has been humiliating to the government."

In one of his articles* Julian attacked Stephen W. Dorsey, late United States Senator from Arkansas, of "Star Route Mail" fraud fame, contending that Dorsey had unlawfully used the homestead and preemption laws to acquire immense tracks of land in the vicinity of the so-called "Una de Gato" Grant in Colfax County, claiming that Dorsey had sent out "squads of henchmen, who availed themselves of the forms of the preemption and homestead laws in acquiring pretended titles, which were conveyed to him, according to arrangements previously agreed upon."

Julian charged that "the grant owners of New Mexico have not yet retired from their field of operations in Congress. They

*Ibid

CLAIMS OF LAND STEALING 129

have their allies in both Houses. Distinguished senators and representatives from some of the great land states of the west are well understood to be in sympathy with S. W. Dorsey, S. B. Elkins, and their confederates and nothing but the dread of the President in his fight against land thieves restrains them from acting openly."

To Julian's outbursts the members of the so-called "land grant ring," Elkins, Catron, Dorsey replied, "politics." To the cry of "politics," Julian called names of men, claimed land grant claimants knew no principles in politics, used either political party at will to further their interests. "The influence of these claimants over the fortunes of New Mexico is perfectly notorious," thundered Julian. "They have hovered over the territory like a pestilence. To a fearful extent they have dominated governors, judges, district attorneys, legislatures, surveyors-general and their deputies, marshals, treasurers, county commissioners, and the controlling business interests of the people. They have confounded political distinctions and have subordinated everything to the greed for land. The continuous and unchecked ascendancy of one political party for a quarter of a century had wrought demoralization in the other. T. B. Catron is a leading Republican, and C. H. Gildersleeve, an equally prominent Democrat, but no political nomenclature fits them. They are simply traffickers in land and recognized captains of this controlling New Mexico industry. This tells the whole story. They have a diversity of gifts, but the same spirit. They are politicians 'for revenue only' and have a formidable following."

Stephen W. Dorsey, then sojourning in New Mexico, was selected as the man to take up the cudgels against Surveyor-General Julian. The North American Review accepted a reply from Dorsey to Julian's articles, and it appeared in that magazine for December, 1887. Dorsey proceeded to say that "Mr. Julian himself had often been charged with being a corruptionist of the worst order." Citing the fact that Julian had been chairman of the Committee of Public Land in the House of Representatives at a time when Congress had voted away to railroad corporations a "larger area of land than would cover all the New England and half the Middlewestern States," Dorsey contended, "land not taken from the sage brush, the cactus and sandhill country," but "the splendid lands of Illinois, Iowa, Minnesota, Northern Michigan, Wisconsin, Eastern Kansas, Dakota and the Southern States of Mississippi, Arkansas, Florida, and Louisiana." Every acre in those states, Dorsey argued, "was worth more than thirty acres in the arid region." Dorsey bluntly charged, "if there has been a land grabber in this country, a man who has done more than any other man to prevent the settlers from exercising their rights under the homestead and preemption laws, Mr. Julian is that man." Dorsey attacked Julian bitterly, claiming that "fifty years ago" he had been elected to office as a pro-slavery Democrat; that he then became a Free Soil leader, then a conservative Whig, remained "bravely at home during the war," became a Republican, was elected to Congress, where he became a zealot of zealots, a destructionist and radical of the bitterest type, as against the southern states and their people." The Republican party then became "too corrupt" for Julian, Dorsey alleged and he became a reformer, attaching himself to the Grover Cleveland cause.

Former Senator Dorsey took issue with Julian on his claims of incompetency, fraud, corruption, misadministration in connection with handling of New Mexico land grants, pointing out the Democratic as well as Republican administration had shared in acts of recommendation, of confirmation, saying that with few exceptions every land grant in New Mexico to which he had referred had been confirmed by Congress prior to 1861.

With reference to the Maxwell Land Grant, Dorsey to some extent agreed with Julian, but pointed out Democratic administrative action. "Julian alludes especially to the Maxwell Grant, which I believe with him," wrote Dorsey, "was never intended

CLAIMS OF LAND STEALING 131

when made to cover the extent of the Territory that is now claimed as included within its borders. That grant, however, was occupied and the natural landmarks were named in the concession. It was reported favorably by a Democratic Surveyor-General. It was approved by Jacob Thompson, who was Democratic Secretary of the Interior. It was confirmed by a Democratic Congress and the Confirmatory Act was approved by Mr. Buchanan, a Democratic President."

Dorsey denied all wrongdoing on his part, defended his acts in connection with acquiring land in New Mexico. His reply was even-tempered, logical, demonstrated a wide grasp of national and territorial affairs. Dorsey did not agree with Julian that land grants should be passed upon by the Secretary of the Interior. He urged the appointment of a tribunal, a special court or commission, with limited authority as to time, for adjudication of land titles in New Mexico. Dorsey's plan, in principle, finally resulted in the Court of Private Land Claims.

In the concluding paragraphs of his reply to Julian, Dorsey discussed not so much land grants and land titles, but what could be done and what should be done with land in New Mexico. Viewed in the light of present day development, Dorsey's views and observations, made more than fifty years ago, demonstrate clear, sound thinking when dealing with the future with reference to rainfall, irrigation works, the livestock industry, and the uses generally to which, in his opinion, public domain and large tracts of privately owned land in New Mexico could be put.

"Land Titles in New Mexico" was the subject of an address by Hon. Frank W. Springer, the retiring president of the New Mexico Bar Association at Santa Fe on January 6, 1890. Springer, using the occasion as a springboard to take the hide off Surveyor-General Julian, began by saying:

> "I have chosen a trite subject for my retiring address, and scarcely expect to contribute anything that is not

already well known to those who listen here . . . But it is one which so far dwarfs all others, in its relation to the interests of this territory, that one hopes by iteration and reiteration, to help a little to engage the attention of the national legislators to the demand of justice for which New Mexico has begged in vain for 25 years."

Continuing Springer said:

"While the man who thought he was a property owner in New Mexico with a legitimate title under Mexico will find in the treaty and the diplomatic assurances and explanatory protocol respecting it, and the early exposition of his status thereunder by the courts, a very interesting treatise upon theoretical private rights, when he wants the use of his land that is a very different thing. The courts cannot recognize his title at all without confirmation by Congress. Congress will not confirm it, nor furnish him any tribunal which can. But whenever a squatter has taken possession of a choice piece of his property, the courts will preserve the status in quo. So he is remitted to seek justice at its original fonts, and the longest rifle holds the ranch."

Frank Springer then went after George W. Julian, United States Surveyor-General, hammer and tongs. Springer said:

"As an illustration of these sweeping accusations, Julian cites the Maxwell Land Grant, which he says 'was an astounding piracy of the public domain,' and intimates that the Commissioner of the General Land Office and the Surveyor-General were corrupt parties to it. He did this in the face of the fact that three months before it was written the Supreme Court of the United States had rendered two elaborate and unanimous decisions upon that very grant, at the end of five years litigation, in which the government at vast expense in procuring testimony and employing counsel, had undertaken by a direct suit to establish the same charges repeated by Julian in the North American Review."

Springer then went on to quote parts of the decision in the Maxwell Land Grant case, 121 U. S. 375, 122 U. S. 375.

Perhaps the best qualified man in New Mexico to speak on the land grant subject, because of his long experience in the Maxwell Land Grant litigation and profound study of the problems involved, Frank W. Springer's address was printed and widely distributed.

"I want to be distinctly understood," continued Springer in his address,

> "The question is not whether we are in favor of grants or not. We all agree that the Territory would be far better off today, if there had not been any. But it is not a question of sentiment we have to deal with; it is an existing fact of overwhelming significance for this region. The grants are here, and they cannot be got rid of by declamation or newspaper headlines. Whether a man is, in the now familiar parlance of this country 'grant or anti-grant,' depends for the most part upon his personal interests. If he has a grant, he wants the grant titles sustained. If he has not, but covets a piece of his neighbor's grant, he wants to see them overthrown. From the point of view of this inquiry, the one is no better nor worse than the other. But upon the broader question, which

goes to the very life of the commonwealth, whether the grant titles shall be speedily settled, there can be no two opinions, if we except the political mountebanks and professional agitators who thrive upon disorders incident to a situation like ours . . . It is not creditable to the United States that after forty years, 150,000 of her people should be left in the midst of chaos, which invites dishonest speculation, turbulence, riot and rebellion; and which repels, worse than any Chinese wall, the coming of industry, capital and intelligence for the honest and permanent development of the country. It is not the grant claimant alone who is affected by the uncertainty that prevails. If he cannot tell what land will ultimately be confirmed to him, the settler, seeking to acquire land upon the public domain, is no better off. He does not know at what moment a tract of land, now supposed to belong to the United States, may be claimed under some hitherto unknown grant, which the courts will ultimately be compelled to recognize. Besides this, the land officers are very fond of assuming judicial functions, and declaring this or that grant is void, opening it to entry as public land, and inviting settlers to locate upon it, who afterwards, when the grant is declared valid by the courts, lose their time, their improvements and opportunities for favorable locations elsewhere, and are without redress from the government."

CHAPTER XV

Judge Vincent and Grover Cleveland

ON October 14, 1885, President Grover Cleveland suspended Chief Justice William A. Vincent, Judge of the First Judicial District of the Territory of New Mexico. Vincent telegraphed the President for a hearing, asked for the cause of his suspension and began to pull every political wire at his command. Not receiving any reply from Cleveland, Vincent wired W. H. Garland, Attorney-General, asking permission to leave at once for Washington from Santa Fe to defend himself in the matter of the suspension. Garland wired back: "I have no permission to give, as your suspension by the President is absolute. Your successor will be appointed within a day or two." Vincent telegraphed to his influential friends in his home state of Illinois, all without the desired result. Cleveland stood pat and another "carpet bagger" had walked the plank to political exile so far as New Mexico was concerned.

Vincent was suspended from office by Cleveland for a single misstep. He had appointed Stephen W. Dorsey, former United States senator from Arkansas as a member of the Colfax County jury commission of five men to select the names of grand and petit jurors. Dorsey had taken up residence in New Mexico only a year or so before. He was known throughout the nation because of his trial in the District of Columbia on "star route" mail fraud charges. Acquitted by a jury he had moved to New Mexico and started a cattle ranch. Nearby ranchers called the place Dorsey's "Castle Ranch."

Vincent's defense of Dorsey's appointment was vigorous. He

claimed that it had never occurred to him that Dorsey's appointment would be objectionable; that before he made the appointment he had consulted Colonel William Breeden, the Attorney-General of New Mexico, with Frank Springer and George W. Prichard, prominent lawyers of the territory, and with W. R. Webb, the clerk of the court. In his defense Judge Vincent pictured conditions at the time in Colfax County as follows:

"There have been for many years a number of turbulent spirits in Colfax County who have continually fomented trouble. Last spring the Sheriff, in attempting to make an arrest, was shot and so badly wounded that he is still confined to his bed. Shortly after this occurrence one of the guilty parties was arrested and placed in jail at Springer, the county seat of Colfax County. A number of his associates attempted to release him from the jail, and in a riot which followed three men were killed, and remarkable as it may seem, a large number of prominent and influential citizens sustained the parties who made the attack on the jail and it was necessary to call on the United States regular troops from Fort Union to quell the riot and preserve the peace. The trouble renewed old feuds, created some years ago, when, on account of similar trouble, it was necessary to annex Colfax County to Taos County for judicial purposes, and the feeling between all classes of people was more bitter than I can describe it or you can imagine it. In addition to this there is a continual war in New Mexico between the sheep men and the cattle men in regard to range and water rights. When the court convened in Colfax County last September there were 168 criminal cases on the docket, and during that time over 100 indict-

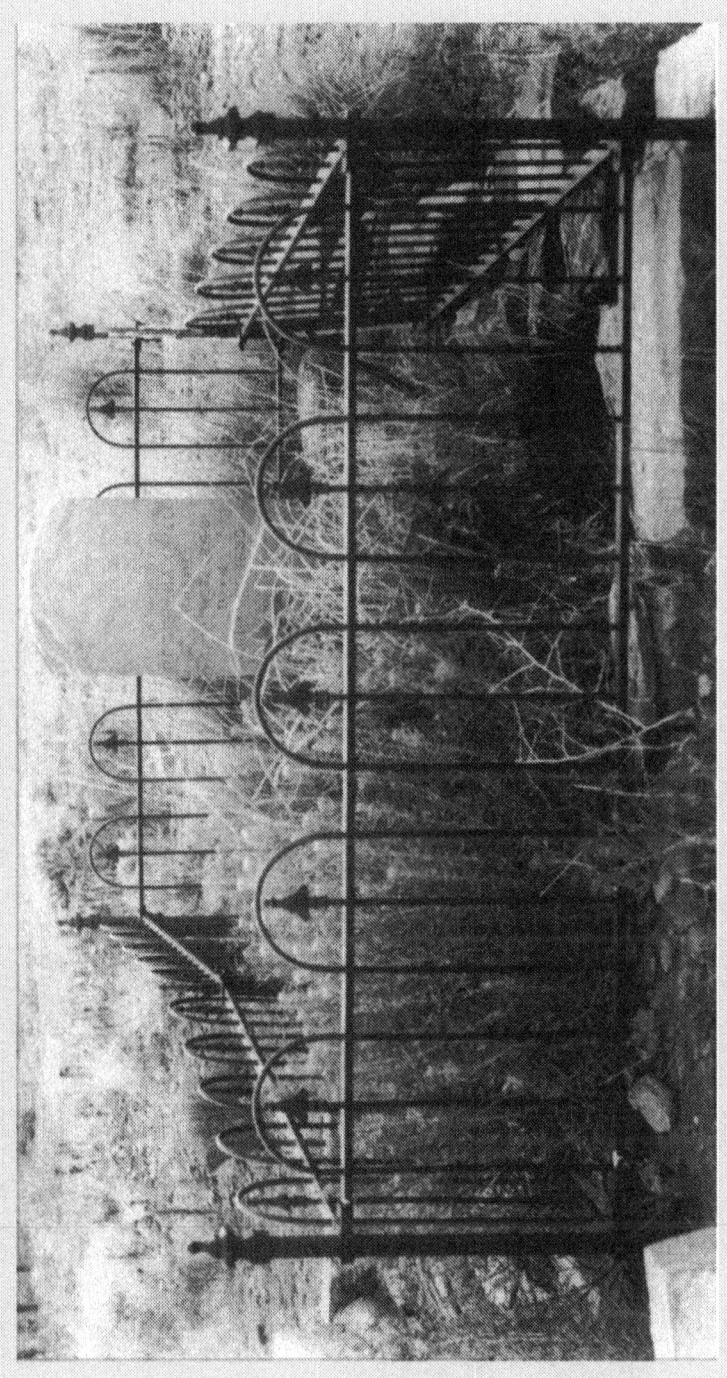

Peter Maxwell Grave at Fort Sumner. Nearby Is the Unmarked Grave of Lucien B. Maxwell

ments were found, many if not all, growing out of the trouble that I have referred to."

Vincent's appeal to President Cleveland was ignored. The greatest obstacle that Vincent had to hurdle, and could not, was that he had accepted an invitation to visit Dorsey's fabulous ranch home, where he had gone with several prominent politicians, and where, his enemies claimed, he had been wined and dined. Subsequent events disclosed that Judge Vincent had been removed as the result of a complaint made by W. P. Fishback, of Indianapolis, Indiana, at the request of his brother-in-law, Rev. O. P. McMains, of Raton, New Mexico. McMains, day in and day out, for many years had fought against the Maxwell Land Grant crowd. Fishback, in a letter addressed to the Indianapolis Journal, November 16, 1885, defending McMains, said:

> "There is no man in Colfax County more respected than Mr. McMains, and at the last election for members of the territorial legislature he was chosen a member of that body in spite of all the money and influence of land thieves and rings. What makes him a 'very dangerous and violent incendiary,' as Judge Vincent calls it, is the fact that owing to his efforts alone Secretary Kirkwood and Attorney General Brewster were induced to bring a suit in the name of the United States in the federal court in Denver to cancel the bogus Maxwell Land Grant patent, by which nearly 2,000,000 acres of the public domain have been stolen."

Judge Vincent made no headway in his demand that Cleveland hold up the suspension and grant him a hearing. The President reached out and touched the shoulder of Judge Elisha V. Long, who was then judge of the circuit court of Whitney

County, Indiana, and named him as Vincent's successor. Judge Long had served as a Judge in Indiana for ten years. He had passed upon the application for admission to the bar of Indiana of Thomas R. Marshall, later to become Vice-President of the United States when Woodrow Wilson was elected President in 1912. Long's farewell to the Bar of Whitney County was indicative of his mental and moral calibre. To quote only one paragraph:

> "It is much easier to have in the mind an ideal court than to manifest it among daily duties. One called upon to decide the rights of men, to stand fair minded, and just, leaning neither to one side nor to the other, cannot have too high a conception of the honorable obligation resting upon him. His conscience cannot be too sensitive, his love of right and fair dealing too strong. Standing between contending parties, clashing and opposing claims, counsel burning with enthusiasm sometimes for an imaginary interest, deeply wounded perhaps at the ruling of the court, and fiery with momentary resentment, it is no easy task to remain calm under quick retort and hold the even balance of mind so essential to correct results. To give ample time for just investigation and yet make proper haste, to give every point full consideration and to important ones careful painstaking examination, to weigh and consider, so that every right shall be properly maintained is a work of large dimensions. All this I have earnestly sought to do, but no doubt have often failed. For the people of this county I cherish the most friendly regard; for the members of the bar, officers and ex-officials of the court, an abiding friendship."

Judge Long, father of Boaz Long, for many years prominent in the United States diplomatic service in South and Central American countries, made his home in Las Vegas, served honorably on the bench and lived far beyond three score and ten.

The Dorsey Ranch, located near the Maxwell Land Grant, was in its day a showplace in New Mexico. The ranch was described in the Las Vegas Gazette of April 26, 1884, as follows:

"The ranch of Dorsey is a large unpretentious adobe building, situated in a wide, shallow arroyo, bordered by cottonwood trees and surrounded by a wire fence. Inside the ranch is furnished magnificently, especially the parlor, Dorsey's sleeping room and the guest rooms for visitors, of which the house has several and which are in constant use. A piano stands in the sitting room which also contains a well selected library and a completely appointed sideboard. Dorsey rises early in the morning, has breakfast and a talk with his foreman and bookkeeper, and then rides ten or fifteen miles over his range. Returning to the ranch he has another meal and then chats and smokes, visits with his guests if he has any, and reads until bedtime which is early now. Sometimes, but rarely, he visits Rocky Crossing, Springer or Raton and now and then takes a flying trip east. He generally dresses in a gray tweed suit, is affable toward all his employes and is popular among neighboring cattlemen, by whom he is generally addressed as 'Senator.' When spoken to on the subject, he invariably insists that he is out of politics and will be in the future simply a cattleman. The range which he occupies is well watered, with good timber and hill shelter, and is so situated that a few miles of fencing will hold many more from the invasion of the cattle of other stockmen, while keeping his own on the range. He manages his cattle matters in a businesslike way, employs an experienced foreman and a bookkeeper, has his own range riders and sign riders and his own round ups. He has had very good luck since he began his cattle enterprise, has lost few cattle, and his herd is rapidly increasing."*

---

*Dorsey, investigated in Washington, D. C., on Star Route charges was vindicated. His enemies claimed that he had become wealthy through Star Route mail contracts. Dorsey's ranch in Colfax County covered about 12,000 acres of patented land, with access to much additional grazing land. He ran about 22,000 cattle at one time. Dorsey was a friend of Robert G. Ingersoll, famous lecturer, who visited the Dorsey Ranch at times. Ingersoll delivered a lecture in Springer on November 10, 1884. Enemies of Dorsey during his residence in New Mexico circulated cards, which they claimed had been printed at the News Office in Oberlin, Ohio, about the year 1860, which read as follows: "Stephen W. Dorsey, house, sign and carriage painter, oak, mahogany, black walnut and maple graining done in the best manner." Robert G. Ingersoll lived part time in New Mexico during 1886 and 1887, was interested in a ranch property and built a house near Chico, in Colfax County. Ingersoll defended Dorsey in the Star Route mail fraud investigation.

CHAPTER XVI
Dawson's Ranch and A. A. Jones

O**N January 17, 1869, Lucien B. Maxwell and Luz B. Maxwell executed a deed naming John B. Dawson grantee, by which they conveyed certain land in Mora County, New Mexico. The deed was witnessed by Chas F. Holly and Jesus G. Abreu and was recorded in Book 2 of Records of Mora County, pages 113 and 114 on February 12, 1869. The consideration expressed in the deed was three thousand seven hundred dollars. Federal revenue stamps in the amount of one dollar fifty cents attached to the deed evidenced the compliance with the laws of the United States of America. The deed conveyed "all the land or ground now suitable for farming or cultivating purposes, in the valley or drainage of the Vermejo River, County of Mora, Territory of New Mexico, beginning at a certain dam, at the head of a certain ditch, at the right hand point of rocks, from thence running down on the north side of said river to a certain other pile of rocks, on a knoll or elevation, with some bushes near thereto; thence running near southward across said river to a pinon tree to the right of a ridge, near a wash, which tree is marked with the letter "L"; thence running up said river on the south side to place of beginning; containing about —— acres, more or less."

This interesting description, certain to send cold chills up and down the spine of a title examiner, to cause the most resourceful pipe-smoking land surveyor to scratch his last match on a worn out pair of corduroy trousers, contained the germ of much litigation. Lucien B. Maxwell had originally contracted to sell the land involved to Miller, Maulding and Curtis, who in turn sold their rights under the contract to Dawson.

In 1870 the Maxwells sold the entire Maxwell Land Grant to a syndicate of capitalists. The transfer of the land from the Maxwells to John B. Dawson a year earlier was excepted in the transaction. It was believed that at the outside the Dawson description called for not more than 1,000 acres. When the litigation was ended the description was good for twenty thousand acres.

Within a few years the Dawson deed of January 17, 1869, was scrutinized very carefully. The description was studied and considered for many hours by lawyers, surveyors and old timers. The reason was that excellent steam coal, in immense quantities, had been discovered on the part of the Maxwell Land Grant that had been conveyed to John B. Dawson.

On May 14, 1888, Andrieus A. Jones, of Las Vegas, was admitted to practice law in the Territory of New Mexico. On October 10, 1891, Attorney Jones, twenty-nine years of age, was in his office dreaming of the carefree days he had spent as a school teacher, wishing that he had never abandoned the certainty of the schoolroom for the uncertainty of the legal profession. The door of the Jones' office was opened and Charles Springer, of Cimarron, walked in quietly and introduced himself. Springer needed no introduction. He was a brother of Frank W. Springer, late of Wapello, Louisa County, Iowa, famous because of his victory in every court in the land from the lowest to the highest in litigation of great importance involving the ownership, extent and validity of the Maxwell Grant. Charles Springer, who had arrived in Cimarron from Iowa on October 26, 1878, in his soft, cautious manner of speaking, told Jones that the Maxwell Land Grant Company was going to bring, or had brought, a suit to eject John B. Dawson from his ranch in Colfax County and that Dawson wanted Jones to represent him in the litigation. Would Jones represent

Dawson? If so, what would Jones charge for the work? Jones was agreeable to the employment, but hesitated about naming a fee. Springer inquired if a fee of five hundred dollars would be satisfactory. Jones hemmed and hedged a bit, but finally agreed to the fee, according to later sworn testimony of Springer. In his testimony in litigation over the fee that later developed Jones did not greatly depart from the story told by Springer, excepting that Jones used the words "case" and "suit" instead of "litigation." Jones contended in his testimony, however, that after the litigation in the Dawson case had been instituted, Springer had said to him: "You cannot be expected to attend to this business for $500; go on with the case, and we will see how it comes out, and after it is all over, you will be paid what is right." Springer paid Jones one hundred dollars on account, promised to take care of map making, procuring and interviewing witnesses and similar work, and left Las Vegas. The battle for the Dawson ranch was on its way and A. A. Jones, although he apparently did not know it, was engaged in a lawsuit of major importance with many ramifications.

The Maxwell Land Grant Company in due time sued Dawson in ejectment. The case was tried before a jury in San Miguel County district court with a verdict favorable to Dawson. The Grant Company appealed to the Territorial supreme court, which affirmed the decision of the court below. Maxwell Land Grant Co. v. Dawson, 7 N. M. 133. The cause was appealed to the Supreme Court of the United States with the result that on February 5, 1894, the judgment of the Territorial supreme court was reversed and the cause was remanded for a new trial. Maxwell Land Grant Co. v Dawson, 151 U. S. 586. The description contained in the deed from Maxwell to Dawson stumped the Supreme Court of the United States. Mr. Justice Brown, who wrote the opinion complained: "It is incredible that any man should have paid $3,700 for such an indefinite purchase of real estate." The case was again tried to a jury and again Dawson prevailed. The Maxwell Land Grant Company removed the case to the Supreme Court of the Territory on appeal, but the appeal was dismissed when Jones pointed out to Frank W. Springer that he could not prevail in that court because of defective assignments or error and because of the state of the record.

Jury trials were over, appeals to Territorial supreme court and Supreme Court of the United States had been disposed of and A. A. Jones was ready to receive his compensation. He approached Springer at various times and was met with the answer that Jones had agreed to take care of the litigation for five hundred dollars, one hundred of which had been paid at the time of the employment, two hundred when Jones went to Washington to argue the case in the Supreme Court of the United States, and one hundred of which had been paid during the course of the trials, leaving one hundred dollars still due. Jones countered with the proposition that subsequent to the time when he got into the case he had learned that Springer had not been frank with him; that he had not told him that the Dawson ranch was a vast coal field, or that he had acquired from the Dawsons on October 29, 1896, a deed to one-half interest in all the sub surface minerals on the ranch, and pointed out to him that on October 3, 1901, the Dawsons and Charles Springer and Mary Chase Springer, his wife, had conveyed the Dawson ranch to the Dawson Fuel Company for four hundred fifty thousand dollars.

Springer, however, was adamant and held to the figure of five hundred dollars, his argument being that a contract was a contract; and that besides he had "thrown" other legal work to Jones, as he had promised to do, during the period covered by the litigation, which had netted Jones over nine thousand dollars. Jones sued Charles Springer and John B. Dawson on August 3, 1901, for seventy-five thousand dollars, alleging this sum was due him for services rendered in the litigation over the

Dawson ranch. The suit was filed in Colfax County, but Springer and Dawson filed an affidavit that they could not get a fair trial in that county, offering supporting affidavits by Christopher N. Blackwell and Robert W. Maize. Justice William J. Mills, on October 8, 1901, granted a change of venue to San Miguel County; an answer was filed by Charles Springer denying all of the allegations of Jones' complaint. Jones had E. A. Fiske of Santa Fe with him on the complaint, but Neill B. Field, of Albuquerque, became the actual trial lawyer in the case for Jones. Thomas B. Catron of Santa Fe became associated as counsel for Charles Springer, but Charles A. Spiess actually tried the case for the defendant.

Jones in his testimony contended that if he had known that Springer was the owner of an undivided one-half interest in the ranch, or of its immense value as coal land he never would have considered accepting the offer of a fee of five hundred dollars suggested by Springer. It became apparent in the course of the testimony that Charles Springer did not want it known that he had an interest in the Dawson ranch because his brother, Frank W. Springer, was a director in the Maxwell Company. Jones testified that he did all of the work of a lawyer in the case, but admitted that Springer had assisted materially in preparing for trial. The peculiar fact developed in the case that Frank W. Springer, brother of Charles Springer, had represented the Maxwell Land Grant Company as chief counsel in prosecuting the ejectment case against Dawson, with Thomas B. Catron of Santa Fe as associate counsel.

Well-known lawyers of the Territory offered the usual expert testimony on the question of fees. Albert B. Fall, who testified that he had been engaged for thirteen years in the practice of law in the Territory, and was for two years an Associate Justice, testified that he had participated in the supreme court in the decision of the Maxwell Land Grant Company case against John B. Dawson. Assuming, Mr. Fall testified, that the land was of the value of four hundred fifty thousand dollars and Springer had received one-half of it for managing the litigation and paying the expenses incident to the same, amounting to some two thousand dollars, then Jones should receive one-half of the amount Springer received in the transaction, which would make Jones' fee one hundred twenty-five thousand dollars, less the cost of the litigation. O. A. Larrazolo testified substantially in the same vein as Fall.

Charles Springer, a witness in his own defense, testified that he was forty-three years old; that since 1878 he had lived in Colfax County, New Mexico, to which place he had come from Iowa. He gave a detailed, specific account of his transaction with Jones; testified that he had conferred many times over a period of some fifteen years with Dawson about the land, its title, its boundaries, the possibilities for coal; that he had made full disclosure of all pertinent facts to Jones at the time of his first interview and testified there never had been any possibility of misunderstanding on the part of Jones. John D. Veeder, an attorney of Las Vegas, testified that Jones' services were worth not more than five thousand dollars. R. E. Twitchell, later to become a noted historian, testified that the services of Jones were worth from twenty-five hundred to thirty-five hundred dollars. Jeremiah Leahy, a lawyer of Raton, fixed the fee at from two to four thousand dollars. The jury, Gomecindo Ortiz, Juan Jose Salazar, Prospero Baca, Clemente Segura, Francisco Wallace, Jesus Maria Romero, Blaz Ortiz, Abado Garcia, Rumaldo Trujillo, David Urioste, Felipe Rivera y Martinez and Jose A. Baca, twelve good men and true, drawn from the citizenry of San Miguel County, brought in a verdict, after a trial of seven days, in favor of the defendant, Charles Springer, and Judge William J. Mills duly noted on the docket that the "defendant shall go hence without day."

The Supreme Court of the Territory affirmed the court below, Joseph M. Cunningham, Trustee, et al, vs. Charles Springer, et al, 13 N. M. 259. A writ of error was sued out to the Supreme Court of the United States, but Springer again prevailed. Cunningham v. Springer, 203 U. S. 647.

After the mandate had come down from the Supreme Court of the United States, after Neill B. Field had huffed and puffed and recovered his inimitable dignity and poise, after A. A. Jones had gone about his way in his ever alluring quest of a toga in the Senate of the United States, in which he was successful many years later, there came an envelope addressed to A. A. Jones, Attorney at Law, Las Vegas, New Mexico, in the personal handwriting of Charles Springer. Jones opened the envelope, took out a check, payable to his order for ten thousand dollars, signed by Charles Springer. Jones looked dreamily out in the direction of the nearby El Porvenir Peak in the mountains he loved so well, let his mind wander for a few moments in retrospection. Then he took the check, tore it into small bits, placed the bits in an envelope addressed to Charles Springer, Attorney at Law, Raton, New Mexico, and mailed it in the postoffice, postage prepaid.

The Dawson Ranch became a great coal field, one of the most important in the entire southwest. Dawson, old time rancher, had been reluctant to sell his property. He had a herd of good cows, sold milk in Raton and the nearby country. Finally he arranged to hold out of the deal what he called the homeplace, containing twelve hundred sixty acres. He had heard the purchaser expected to mine coal and proposed to build a coal mining town. He wanted to perpetuate his name in the region and the purchasers agreed to call the town after him. Mrs. Dawson, unable to fully realize the fact that she and her husand would soon be in possession of a quarter of a million dollars for their share of the property, did a little trading on her own before she signed the deed. She demanded that she should have the exclusive right for a period of ten years to sell milk in the new mining camp to be known as Dawson. The purchasers agreed to this demand. Mrs. Dawson signed the deed. Many years later one of the old time characters in the vicinity remarked that if A. A. Jones had been as careful in trading with Charley Springer about his fee as Mrs. Dawson had been with the fuel company in trading about her milk concession, there would have been no lawsuit over lawyer fees.

CHAPTER XVII
"Steve" Elkins and "Tom" Catron

STEPHEN BENTON ELKINS, who was intimately connected with the financing of the Maxwell Land Grant & Railway Co., and who was censured because his brother, John T. Elkins, was one of the surveyors of the Maxwell Land Grant, had a most amazing career. Born in Perry County, Ohio, September 6, 1841, Elkins died January 4, 1911. He was graduated from the University of Missouri in 1860, taught school for a short time before engaging in the Civil War on the Union side, in just what capacity has never been clear. Elkins was captured by Quantrell's band of guerillas, charged with being a Union spy. Quantrell ordered him shot, but Elkins' life was saved by two young men, whom he had taught in school—Cole Younger and Jim Younger, who later went to the penitentiary in Minnesota for their misdeeds, and for whom, in later years, Elkins repeatedly asked a pardon. Arriving in New Mexico late in 1863, Elkins settled at Mesilla, was admitted to the New Mexico Bar on June 6, 1864, learned the Spanish language, was elected to the Legislature in 1866, appointed by President Andrew Johnson, United States District Attorney for New Mexico in 1868; elected president of the First National Bank of Santa Fe in 1871, succeeding Lucien B. Maxwell, serving in that capacity for thirteen years. In 1873 and again in 1875, Elkins was elected Delegate in Congress from New Mexico. While in Congress on August 12, 1876, Elkins obtained from President U. S. Grant an executive order abrogating the treaty with the Jicarilla Apaches, which had assigned to them that portion of New Mexico north of the San Juan River and east of the Navajo reservation; and on August 18, 1876, was successful in having the Post Office Department step up mail service from Trinidad to Santa Fe from fifty-seven hours to forty hours.

Elkins was married at the Franklin Street Presbyterian Church, Baltimore, Maryland, on April 14, 1875, to Miss Hallie L. Davis, a daughter of Henry Gassaway Davis, then United States Senator from West Virginia. Elkins and his bride went to Europe on a wedding trip, but Elkins devoted much of his time abroad to getting capital to build a railroad to Cimarron, and the Maxwell Land Grant country. Elkins had been busy in Congress on statehood for New Mexico, but apparently courting Miss Davis and trying to get a bill through for New Mexico's statehood were too much for him. On February 20, 1875, the Las Vegas Gazette said editorially:

> "After we had already set up in solid matter the synopsis of the Enabling Act to let our readers know on what conditions our Territory was to be admitted to the Union as a state, here comes flashing over the wires that Colorado was admitted, but that New Mexico was left out in the cold. Nothing in God's world could be advanced to wash off the stain of Mr. Elkins' character as a delegate. His inability and thorough incapacity as a representative were shown to the world in their full light and the people of New Mexico ought to be congratulated that his term of office has expired."

Elkins, however, was reelected to Congress while abroad, having been nominated by the Republican party in Santa Fe on June 1, 1875. Elkins wrote in his letter of acceptance of the nomination to William Breeden, Chairman of the party in New Mexico, from Amsterdam, Holland:

"Since going to Washington eighteen months since, I am convinced that there is no place like New Mexico to live in; it is there that I have established myself and there that I expect to live the balance of my life."

The results of the election for delegate, held on September 25, 1875, were: Elkins, 8,376; Valdez, 6,887, majority for Elkins, 1,489. Elkins' marriage into the family of Henry Gassaway Davis proved to be his entrance into the national political arena and gradually he retired from the political scene in New Mexico. In 1884 he became chairman of the executive committee of the National Republican Committee, was largely responsible for bringing about the nomination of James G. Blaine in 1884, and for his services in helping Benjamin Harrison to be elected to the presidency, Elkins was named Secretary of War in the Harrison cabinet in 1891, serving until he was elected United States Senator from West Virginia in 1894. In the national capital Stephen Benton Elkins became a powerful, nationally known figure. Always a great manipulator, and having extended to him through the Henry Gassaway Davis land, timber, coal and railroad interests in West Virginia, the opportunity to make great sums of money, Elkins was lavish in his spending. He built a magnificent home on the side of a mountain in West Virginia, called for his wife, Halliehurst, a property that later went to Davis and Elkins college. In Washington, the Elkins built a mansion at 1626 K Street, now demolished, which was one of the show places of the capital, with its magnificent paintings by Sir Joshua Reynolds, and many another artist; its solid gold dinner service. It was at this mansion that Duke d'Abruzzi, Italian nobleman, courted Katherine Elkins, beautiful daughter of the Elkins. For a time in New Mexico Stephen B. Elkins was a law partner of Thomas Benton Catron. Both Elkins and Catron had been given the name Benton, after Thomas Benton,

United States Senator from Missouri. Elkins and Catron had been classmates at the University of Missouri.

Born in La Fayette County, Missouri, on October 6, 1840, Catron enlisted in the Confederate Army at the outbreak of the Civil War, fought in many battles, was induced to come to New Mexico from Missouri by Elkins after the war in 1866, when Elkins was in Missouri on a visit. Elkins and Catron drove across the plans from Missouri to New Mexico, the trip requiring six weeks. Before leaving Missouri, Catron purchased a Spanish grammar, studied it at campfires by night, and was speaking the language on his arrival in the Territory. Once in New Mexico Catron went to Rio Arriba County, remained there two months, until he had perfected himself in Spanish by conversing with natives. He learned that the Republicans were in power politically. Catron joined the Republican party, became one of its most powerful leaders. Like Elkins, Catron was ambitious and a money maker. He went to the New Mexico Legislature, to the National Congress as a delegate, was one of the important attorneys employed by the Maxwell Land Grant Company in its extensive litigation. Throughout his life in New Mexico Catron wielded more power than any other single individual in the Territory. Through land grant litigation and by purchases he acquired more than one million acres of land and at one time was paying six per cent interest on a million dollars that he had borrowed to finance his enterprises. Elkins and Catron had formed a resolution when crossing the plains from Missouri to New Mexico in 1866, that they would both go to the United States Senate. Elkins was elected United States Senator from West Virginia by vote of the legislature in 1894, when about fifty-five years old. Tom Catron was obliged to wait until 1912, when he was elected to the United States Senate from New Mexico, by act of its first state legislature. He was then seventy-one years old. His old time companion, former law partner and bosom friend, Stephen Benton Elkins, however, had been unable to wait for Catron's coming to the Senate. Elkins had passed away on January 4, 1911.

Stephen Benton Elkins and Thomas Benton Catron knew much about the affairs of the Maxwell Land Grant in the hectic days in New Mexico that followed the American Occupation. But they were at the time interested in many New Mexico land grants and doubtless paid but slight attention to its past history or to the stirring events that occurred during the time of their participation in its difficulties.

Many actors played a part in the drama that was the Maxwell Land Grant — Governor Armijo, Carlos Beaubien, Guadalupe Miranda, Padre Martinez, Charles Bent, Lucien B. Maxwell and a host of other men prominent in early day New Mexico affairs.

Padre Antonio Jose Martinez, the Curate of Taos, from the standpoint of the Indians and early day settlers, and Thomas Benton Elkins, Thomas Benton Catron or Frank W. Springer, from the standpoint of the owners, could have written the real story of the Maxwell Land Grant.

Sources

To a large extent the material for this book has been sought in unpublished sources, and in the following pages the more important groups of such sources are indicated.

* * *

(A)
NEWSPAPERS AND PERIODICALS

Cimarron News and Press—January 28, 1876.
Indianapolis Journal (letter of W. P. Fishback)—November 16, 1885.
Las Vegas Gazette (Summary of Indian situation)—October 5, 1872; February 20, 1875; July 26, 1875 (on Lucien B. Maxwell); December 25, 1875; February 12, 1876; September 30, 1876; October 7, 1876; April 6, 1878; March 25, 1880; April 12, 1884; April 26, 1884 (Dorsey Ranch); May 28, 1884.
New Mexico Union (published in Santa Fe)—October 1, 1872.
NORTH AMERICAN REVIEW, Vol. 145 (July to December, 1887) pp 17-31 (Land Frauds).
Raton Comet—February 27, 1885.
TEXAS LAW QUARTERLY, October 1929, pp 154-169, (Law of the New Mexico Land Grant by W. A. Keleher).
The Regimental Flag (an army paper published in Santa Fe)

* * *

(B)
PUBLIC DOCUMENTS AND RECORDS

Act of July 22, 1854 (creating the office of Surveyor-General of New Mexico, United States Statutes at Large, Vol. X, page 309.
An Act to Establish a Court of Private Land Claims, enacted March 3, 1891.
Act of Congress approved June 21 1860 entitled AN ACT TO CONFIRM CERTAIN PRIVATE LAND CLAIMS IN THE TERRITORY OF NEW MEXICO, 12 Statutes at Large 71.
Constitution of the United States, Article 4, Section 1 providing "The Congress shall have power to dispose of all needful rules and regulations respecting the territory or other property, belonging to the United States."
House Resolution No. 1824, 52d Congress, 1st Session (Maxwell Grant thrown open to preemption settlement).
Memorial of New Mexico Legislature to Congress January 6, 1852.
Message of the President of the United States to Congress, December 1, 1889.
Miscellaneous Document No. 201, 49th Congress, 1st Session; (Maxwell Grant thrown open to preemption settlement).
Private Land Claim No. 15 (Maxwell Land Grant Claim).
Decree of the Mexican Congress of 1824, Article 12 (in regard to land grants; that the grants were to be made to "empresarios, for them to colonize with many families."
Farewell address of Judge Elisha V. Long to Whitney County (Indiana) Bar.
Land Titles in New Mexico—by Hon. Frank W. Springer.
Opinion of Judah P. Benjamin, January 18, 1871.
Records of the County Clerk and District Clerk of Colfax County.
Records of County Clerk of Mora County.
Recopilacion de Los Indias, Law 66, Title 2, Book 3.
Recopilacion de Los Indias, Book IV, Title XII, Law X.
Report of the Acting Commissioner of Indian Affairs—1867 (Report of A. B. Norton directed to N. G. Taylor, Commissioner of Indian Affairs).
Report of Commissioner of Indian Affairs for 1872 (Report of Nathaniel Pope).
Report of the Condition of Indian Tribes pp 358 and 486—Government Printing Office, 1867 (Padre Martinez letters).
Report, Commissioner of Private Lands, 52d Congress, 1st Session, No. 1824 accompanying Miscellaneous Document 305, July 9, 1892 (Conspiracy of Elkins, Catron and Williamson).

Reports of the Governors of New Mexico to the Secretary of the Interior for the years 1881, 1882, 1885, 1889.
Report of House Committee on Private Land Claims of the 36th Congress.
Report of Secretary of Interior 1895-1896, p. 498.
Report of B. M. Thomas to Commissioner of Indian Affairs—August 20, 1877.
Treaty of Guadalupe Hidalgo.
U. S. G. S. ANNUAL REPORT, Appendix JJ for 1876, by George M. Wheeler.
U. S. G. S. Bulletin 620 N. (The Aztec Gold Mine, Baldy, New Mexico—by Willis T. Lee, 1916).
United States Statutes at Large, Vol. X, page 309 (Act Creating Office of Surveyor-General of New Mexico).

(c)
TABLE OF CASES CITED

Charles Bent et al. vs. Maxwell Land Grant & Railway Company, 3 New Mexico Reports (Johnson) 159; 3 New Mexico Reports (Gildersleeve) 227.

Charles Bent et al., v. Guadalupe Miranda et al., 8 New Mexico Reports (Gildersleeve) 78.

Cunningham, Joseph M., Trustee, v. Charles Springer et al., 13 New Mexico Reports (Abbott) 259; 203 United States Supreme Court Reports 647; 51 Law Edition, 662.

Maxwell Land Grant Company v. John B. Dawson, 7 New Mexico Reports (Gildersleeve) 133; 151 United States Supreme Court Reports, 586; 38 Law Edition, 279.

Maxwell Land Grant case, 121 United States Supreme Court Reports, 325, 30 Law Edition, 949; 122 United States Supreme Court Reports, 375, 30 Law Edition, 1211.

Maxwell Land Grant & Railway Company et al. v. Guadalupe Thompson, Administratrix, et al., 8 New Mexico Reports (Gildersleeve) 91.

Thompson, Guadalupe, Administratrix, et al. v. The Maxwell Land Grant & Railway Company et al., 3 New Mexico Reports (Johnson) 269; 3 New Mexico Reports (Gildersleeve) 448; 95 United States Supreme Court Reports, 391; 24 Law Edition, 481.

United States v. Maxwell Land Grant Co. and others, 26 Federal Reporter, 118.

United States v. The Maxwell Land-Grant Company et al., 121 United States Supreme Court Reports, 325; 30 Law Edition, 949.

United States v. Maxwell Land-Grant Company et al., 122 United States Supreme Court Reports, 365; 30 Law Edition, 1211.

(D)
REFERENCES TO PUBLISHED VOLUMES

Bancroft, Vol. 27, Arizona and New Mexico pp 666 and 736 (Bancroft's views of Utes and Jicarilla Apaches).

Hall's MEXICAN LAW, 1881.

HISTORY OF NEW MEXICO, SPANISH AND ENGLISH MISSIONS OF THE METHODIST EPISCOPAL CHURCH, Vol. 1, Rev. Thomas Harwood, El Abogado Press, Albuquerque, 1908.

Hodge's Handbook of American Indians, Part 1, p. 915—(comments on tribal background of Utes ["Moache Utes"]).

LIFE EXPLORATIONS AND PUBLIC SERVICES OF JOHN CHARLES FREMONT, Boston, 1856—Upham.

NARRATIVE OF THE EXPLORING EXPEDITION to the ROCKY MOUNTAINS in 1842 and to OREGON and NORTH CALIFORNIA in the YEARS 1843-1844, by Brevet Captain J. C. Fremont, D. Appleton & Co., New York 1846.

New Mexico Court of Private Land Claims, Vols. 1 and 2.

Spanish and Mexican Land Laws by Matthew G. Reynolds, Santa Fe, New Mexico, August 15, 1895.

TRAVELS IN THE GREAT WESTERN PRAIRIES, Thomas J. Farnham, 1843 (REPORT of J. C. FREMONT to Col. J. J. Abert, March 1, 1843).

UPHAM'S LIFE—by Fremont.

Index

Abreu, Jesus G., 43, 141.
Abreu, Petra Beaubien, Conveys to Lucien B. Maxwell, 43.
Act of Congress, approved June 21, 1860 (Confirming Private Land Claims), 19, 110.
Act of Congress of July 22, 1854 (Creating office of Surveyor-General) 126.
Act of Congress, June 21, 1860 (Confirming Maxwell Land Grant), 115.
Act of Congress—1861—straightening line between New Mexico and Colorado, 21.
Adverse Possession—Title claimed by, 119.
Agriculture Industry, 21.
Ahogadera, 90.
Ainsworth, Thos.—Raton Vigilantes, 102.
Alcalde's Party setting up monument, 95.
Allison Brothers—Settling in Cimarron on Maxwell Land Grant, 80.
Allison, Clay, Civil War, 79; Killing of Pancho Griego, 79; noted bad man, 68.
Allison, John, 79; wounding of, 80.
Allison, R. C. (Clay), 79.
Alvord, M., 16.
American capitalists, 22.
American Occupation, 18, 86.
Amos, Half-breed, 94.
Amsterdam, 114, 117.
An Act to Confirm Private Land Claims in the Territory of New Mexico, June 21, 1860. 12 Stat. at Large, 71, 19, 110.
Anderson, A. W.—English Consul, 117.
Antelope, 22.
Anti-Grant Cause, 84.
Anti-Grant Journal, 84.
Anti-Grant meeting, 84.
Anti-Grant men—Colfax County, 24; Line of attack—to go into politics, 85; Raton, 99.
Anti-Grant people — resistance to authority, 106.
Apache Jicarillas 48.
Apaches, 76; Headquarters near Maxwell Ranch, 30; Report on Plight by A. B. Norton, 53; United States Army resolve to exterminate, 50; Whiskey trade with, 46.
Arapahoes, 90.
Arellano, Anastacio, 120.
Arellano, Jesus Maria, 84, 120.
Arellano, Manuel, 120.
Armijo, Governor Manuel, 13, 21, 30, 114, 120.
Arny, W. F. M.—Lease with Lucien B. Maxwell, 46.
Atchison, Topeka & Santa Fe, 72.
Atkinson, Henry M.—Surveyor-General of U. S., Contract with Elkins and Marmon for survey of Grant, 88.
Austin, C. B., 73.
Axtell, Governor S. B., 76.
Axtell, Judge Samuel B.—bench warrant for George Curry, 106; issuance of temporary injunction, 121.
Aztec Mine—Notes, 34.
Baca, Jose A., 146.
Baca, Prospero, 146.
Bancroft, Vol. 27, Arizona and New Mexico, pp 666 and 736 (Bancroft's Views of Utes and Jicarilla Apaches)—Notes, 49.
Barclay's Old Fort, 93.
Barela, Juan, 59.
Barlow, Sanderson & Co.—owners of Mail & Express, 71, 72.
Bayne, Charles M.—Report in litigation, special master, 121.
Bear, 22.
Beaubien, Carlos (Charles), 13, 25, 22, 26, 30, 42, 93, 94, 114; Conveys to Lucien B. Maxwell, 43; Death of, 26; Judge, New Mexico Civil Court, 26, 94; Letter from Guadalupe Miranda, 40; Youth, 25.
Beaubien, Charles (Carlos), 25, 42, 93; Conveys to Lucien B. Maxwell, 43; Letter from Guadalupe Miranda, 40; Youth, 25.
Beaubien, Charles Hipolite Trotier, 25.
Beaubien, Don Carlos—interest in the Grant, 26.
Beaubien, Eleanor, Conveys to Lucien B. Maxwell, 43.
Beaubien Grant, 11.
Beaubien, Juana, Conveys to Lucien B. Maxwell, 43.
Beaubien, Judge, 94.

Beaubien, Luz, 25.
Beaubien, Maria Paula, Conveys to Lucien B. Maxwell, 43.
Beaubien, Narcisse, 27.
Beaubien, Paul, Conveys to Lucien B. Maxwell, 43.
Beaubien, Teodorita, Conveys to Lucien B. Maxwell, 43.
Benedict, Judge Kirby, Order in Charles Bent-Maxwell litigation, 39.
Benjamin, Judah P.—No idea of immense tract of Grant land, 115; Opinion on title to Maxwell Land Grant, 114, 115; Opinion of January 18, 1871, 116.
Bennet, Col. J. F., 72.
Bent, Alfred, 39, 40.
Bent, Charles, Notes, 15, 16, 92, 95; Associate of Lucien B. Maxwell, 27; Fractional interest in Maxwell Grant, 39.
Bent, George, 92.
Bent, Guadalupe, 39.
Bent, Robert, 92.
Bent, William, 92.
Benton, Thomas, 151.
Benton, Tom, 72.
Bentley, J. A., 109; Brief on appeal of Grant litigation, 118.
Bent's Old Fort, 92.
Bernalillo County—in Grant, 6.
Billy the Kid, 30, 38, 67; Deluvina Maxwell, 35.
Black, John—negro, 69.
Black Lake Country, 22.
Blackwell, Christopher N., 145.
Blaine, James G., 151.
Blossburg, 106.
Bonney, William H., 30, 67.
Bosque Redondo, 50.
Bradley, General, 105.
Bransford, Judge, 90.
Breeden, William, 136, 150; Attorney General, 77.
Brewer, Judge—Decision in Grant case, 97.
British capitalists, 22.
Brown, Justice—Opinion in Maxwell Land Grant Co. v. Dawson, 143.
Buchanan, President, 131.
Buenos Aires (Rio de la Plata), 3.
Buffalo, 22.
Burch, Rev. E., 106.
Bustes, Candelaria, 77.
Cameron, ejectment suit against, 119.
Canyon de Chelly, 35.
Cardenas, Manuel, 78.
Carenias, Jose Maes, 77.
Carillo, Sisto, 120.
Carleton, General James H., 51; Feeding the Indians, 53; Letter to Kit Carson, 52; Urging Purchase of Maxwell Land Grant for Indians, 53.
Carleton, Brigadier-General James H., 49.
Carpenter, George P., 116.
Carson, Christopher (Kit), 27; Notes, 27; 28; associate of Lucien B. Maxwell, 27, 28; conference with Lucien B. Maxwell, 51; expedition against Kiowas and Comanches, 52; expedition against Plains Indians, 52; grave of, 72, 73; letter from General Carleton, 51, 52; testimony of Calvin Jones, 88; statement re Utes and Jicarillas, 50; views on Indian troubles, 49; views on purchase of Maxwell Land Grant for Indians, 54; characteristics, 65.
Carson, Kit (See Christopher Carson).
Cashmore, George, 77.
Cashmore, Sacramento, 77.
Casias, Dolores, 120.
Catron, Thomas Benton, 96, 129, 153; Attorney, for Maxwell Land Grant Company; comes to New Mexico; Delegate to Congress, early life of, 152; Law partner of Elkins, 151; Named after Thomas Benton, 151; Ownership of land, 152; Power in New Mexico, 152; purchase of Maxwell's interest in First National Bank of Santa Fe, 36; purchaser of tax sale of Grant, 117; elected from New Mexico to U. S. Senate, 152; special counsel to prosecute Curry, 106; suit against settlers, 120; U. S. Attorney for N. M., alleged conspiracy, 82.
Chacuaco, 89.
Chaffee, Jerome B.—agreement for purchase of Maxwell Grant, 113.
Chaperito, 73.
Charles V, 3.
Chavez, Don Mariano, 17.
Chicarica Mesa, 89, 94.
Chico, Notes, 140.
Chilcott, George M.—agreement for purchase of Maxwell Grant, 113.
Chile, 3.
Choco, 89.
Choco Rico, 89.
Cimarron, 21, 26, 67; building of, 29; Indians, 30; Indians in 1875, 59; Indian Agency discontinued, 54; Indians at Agency described by Las Vegas Gazette, 63; Killing of Pancho Griego by Allison, 79; meetings to raise funds for carrying on suit to test validity of Grant's title, 84; not considered suitable for Indians, 55; important stop for stagecoach, 71; railroad to, 150;

Squatters' Club, 84; Visit of William Vandever, 62; Withdrawal of Indians, 65.
Cimarron News and Elizabeth City Railway Press and Telegraph, 68.
Cimarron News and Press, 69.
Cimarron River, 120.
Civil War—Troubles with Indians, 49.
Claim No. 15—Maxwell Land Grant claim, 115.
Cleveland, President Grover, 125; Appointment of Judge Elisha V. Long, 137; Suspension of Chief Justice Vincent, 135.
Clouthier, Joseph, 43.
Coal, steam—discovered on Maxwell Land Grant, 142.
Cobra, 73.
Colfax County — as pictured by Judge Vincent, 136; created, 21; Grant and anti-Grant camps, 24; Grant owned by citizens of Mexico, 6; Repeal of law attaching to Taos County, 77; Sheriff, 69; suit filed by Maxwell Land Grant Company, 120; Territory embraced within, 3; Una de Gato Grant, 128.
Colonists—need of water, Hostile Indians, 6.
Colonization Law of Mexico, 5.
Colonization of New Mexico, 3.
Colorado, 21, 86.
Colorado-New Mexico line, straightened out by Act of Congress, 21.
Comanche Indians—Hard-pressed by men from Texas, 57.
Comanche Indian-Trade, 57.
Comanches, 49, 51.
Commissioner of Indian Affairs, 54, 61, 62; Urged to buy Maxwell Land Grant for Indians, 53.
Commissioner of Public Lands—Action in opening Grant as public land, 119.
Company "H," 72; organization—abandonment, 100.
Congress of United States, Act of July 22, 1854, 126; Confirmation of Land Grants, 11; Confirming Maxwell Grant, 19; operations of Grant Owners in, 128.
Constable Carter, 103.
Constitution of the United States, Article 4, Section 1, 110.
Cooley, Ex-Commissioner, disapproval of feeding of Indians, 53.
Cordoba, Juan, 120.
Cordova, Mateo, 120.
Count Van Limburg-Stirum, 117.
Court of Private Land Claims, 125;

Cow Creek, 102.
Coyote, 22.
Crocker, Brigadier General, 51.
Crockett, David, killing negro soldiers, 69.
Crops, plan for cultivation, 14.
Crow's Creek, 89.
Cuba, 3.
Cunningham, Joseph M. et al. vs. Charles Springer et al., 13 N.M. 259, 147.
Cunningham v. Springer, 203 U.S. 647, 147.
Curate of Taos, 15, 17, 120.
Curry, George—Chief of Police in Manila, 101; governor of New Mexico, Captain in U.S. Army in Cuba, 101; President Roosevelt, 101; death of brother John, 105; in Raton, 100; leadership displayed, 101; surrender of Jim Masterson, 102; William Howard Taft, 101.
Curry, John—shot by Jesse Lee, 104.
Curtis, George T.—opinion on title to Maxwell Land Grant, 114.
D'Abruzzi, Duke, 151.
Davis, Hallie L., 150.
Davis, Henry Gassaway, 150.
Davis, President Jefferson, 114.
Dawson, John B.—homeplace, perpetuation of name, 147.
Dawson, Mrs. John B.—Sale of milk in Dawson Mine Camp, 147, 148.
Dawson, Will D.—editor, 68.
Dawson Fuel Company, purchase of Dawson Mine, 144.
Dawson Mine, 147; acreage, 142; conveyance by Maxwell to Dawson, 141; deed, 142; description contained in deed, 141; litigation, 142; appeals, Counsel, 143; facts developed in ejectment suit, 145; purchase from Dawsons and Springers, 144; sale of milk, 147, 148.
Dawson Ranch, 141, 147.
Deacy, Estefano, 120.
Democratic party, 26.
Department of Interior, survey of Maxwell Grant, 23.
Department of Missouri, 71.
De Sarlangre, A. A., 117.
Deer, 22.
Dodds, John, 103.
Doolittle, J. R., Report on military expenditures for Indian Affairs, 47.
Dorsey, Stephen W., 128, 129, 130; attack by Julian, 128; attack on Julian, 129; cause of suspension of Chief Justice Vincent, 135; complaint against Indians, 61; defense of his acts acquiring land in New Mexico, 131; letter to Carl

Schurz complaining of Utes and Apaches—October 1, 1877, 61; Star Route, 135; Notes, 140.
Dorsey's Castle Ranch, 135.
Dorsey Ranch, 139.
Doyle, Joe, 91.
Duke d'Abruzzi, 151.
Dutch capitalists, 22.
Eagle's Nest, 89.
Education in New Mexico, 1875, 71.
Ejectment suits, 84, 119.
Elkins and Catron, 36, 152.
Elkins, John (Elkins, John T.), 87, 88, 94, 96.
Elkins, John T., surveyor of Maxwell Land Grant, 149.
Elkins, Katherine, 151.
Elkins, Stephen Benton, 87, 88, 96, 129, 149; alleged conspiracy—Delegate to Congress from N.M., 82; bondsman for Marmon and John T. Elkins, 88; capture by Quantrell's Band, 149; death of, 149, 153; Delegate in Congress from New Mexico, 149; homes of, 151; marriage of, 150; Maxwell Land Grant interests, 58; Memorial of N.M. Legislature of 1874; named after Thomas Benton, 151; obtaining capital for railroad, 150; President of First National Bank of Santa Fe, 149; purchase of Maxwell's interest in First National Bank of Santa Fe, 36; re-election to Congress, 150; rescue by Younger brothers, 149; Secretary of War in Harrison cabinet, 151; Statehood for New Mexico, 150; United States District Attorney, 149; U. S. Senator, 152; Valdez election results in 1875, 151.
Elkins-Marmon survey, 117.
Elkins' Ranch, 37.
Elkins Survey, 117, **118**.
Elizabeth City, 68.
Elizabethtown, gold, 67; water to, 37.
El Moro, 94.
El Paso (formerly Franklin), 40, 42, 102.
El Porvenir Peak, 147.
Empresarios—land grants to, 5, 110.
England—investing public in, 114.
Evarts, Wm. M.—opinion on title to Maxwell Land Grant, 114.
Fairbank, N. K., 116, 117.
Fall, Albert B., testimony in Jones-Springer fee case, 145.
Farmers' Loan and Trust Company of New York, 114.
Feber, Chas.—Town marshal—Las Animas, killing of by Allison brothers, 80.

Federal government, dealings with Maxwell Land Grant, 86; expense of mail route, Vegas to Vinita, 74; failure to buy Grant from Lucien B. Maxwell, 65; opportunity to solve difficulties by acquiring Grant by purchase, 86.
Ferdinand II of Spain, 3.
Fernandez, Andres, 120.
Fernandez, Manuel, 120.
Field, Neill B., 145, 147.
First National Bank of Santa Fe—Notes, 36; capital invested by Lucien B. Maxwell, 36; sale of Lucien B. Maxwell interest to Elkins, president, 149.
Fish, 22.
Fishback, M. P.—Complaint against Judge Vincent, 137; defense of Rev. McMains, 137.
Fiske, E. A., 145.
Fort Bascom, 52, 72, 73.
Fort Bayard, 72.
Fort Elliott, 73.
Fort Garland, 95.
Fort Selden, 72.
Fort Sill, 37.
Fort Sumner, 30, 36, 50, 55; Lucien B. Maxwell, 36.
Fort Union, 23, 67, 72, 105.
Fort Wingate, 72.
Fountain Quibouille, 93;
Franklin, now El Paso, 40.
Fremont, 72; expeditions, 28; Bill Williams, 28; fur trade, 90.
Gable, T. P.—Raton Vigilantes, 102, 105.
Gale, Ira, 106.
Gallinas, 73.
Garcia, Abado, 146.
Garland, W. H., Attorney-General, 135.
Garrett, Patrick F., 30.
Garrick's Hall, 68.
Gast, Charles E., 109.
Geer, George W.—Raton Vigilantes, 102.
Gildersleeve, C. H., 129.
Gold, 67.
Moreno Valley, 34.
Gonzales, Manuel, 120.
Granada, 72.
Grant men—Colfax County, 24.
Grant, President U. S., 149; abrogation of treaty with Jicarilla Apaches; proclamation of August 1, 1875, opening Indian land for settlement, 64.
Grant Ring, 127.
Grant Surveyors, 87.
Greenhorn, 94.
Griego, Francisco (Pancho) killing of by Clay Allison, 79.

Grouse, 22.
Guadalupe-Hidalgo Treaty, 19, 126; Article 8, 6; ratification of, 6.
Guatemala, 3.
Guerillas, Quantrell's Band of—Capture of Stephen Benton Elkins, 149.
Gutierrez, Jose, 120.
Gutierrez, Miguel, 120.
Hall, F. A. Van, 117.
Halliehurst, 151.
Harrison, Benjamin, 151.
Harwood, Rev. Thomas, 31, 33, 75; marriage of Virginia Maxwell, 31.
Hatcher, 94.
Hawkins, John, 95.
Hecklin, Estefena Bent, 39.
Heffron, Gus—Killing negro soldiers, 69.
Hendelong, John, 84.
Herndon, J. E. — Masterson pulls gun on, 100.
Herrera, Anastacio de, 120.
Herrera, Cristobal de, 120.
Herrera, Juan P., 120.
Herrera, Luis de, 120.
Herrera, Miguel, 120.
History of New Mexico, Spanish and English Missions of the Methodist Episcopal Church, Vol. 1, Rev. Thomas Harwood, El Abogado Press, Albuquerque, 1908—Notes, 31.
Hixenbaugh, Deputy Duce, 104.
Hodge's Handbook of American Indians, Part 1, p. 915—"Moache Utes."
Holbrook, Joseph, 84.
Holland—investing public in, 114.
Holly, Charles F.—Notes, 36, 141; agreement for purchase of Maxwell Grant, 113.
Homesteaders, discouraged from taking up land in N.M., 24.
Hooper, Henry M.—Notes, 36.
Houghton, Wheaton and Smith, 18.
House Committee on Private Land Claims of the 36th Congress, 127.
Howe, John, 104.
Huerfano, 93.
Hunt, Charles F.—Raton Vigilantes, 102, 105.
Indian Agency, Cimarron — discontinued, 60.
Indians, 45, 65, 67; condition cited by New Mexico Legislature of 1874, 55; consider Miranda-Beaubien Grant theirs, 22; expense of attempt to subdue, 47; economic problems, 60; New Mexico Legislature's Memorial regarding, 55; plan to have them live on Maxwell Grant proved a failure, 60; Ration day, 32; reason for removal from Taos, 46; removal from Maxwell Land Grant, 61; situation reviewed by Father Antonio Jose Martinez, 47; suffer from lack of rations, 30; troubles during Civil War, 49; views of Padre Martinez, 48.
Ingersoll, Robert G.—Lecture in Springer—Notes, 140.
Irvine, A. G.—Indian Agent at Cimarron, 59.
Iturbide—Establishing independence of Mexico, 5.
Jicarilla Apaches, 45, 107; Abrogation of treaty with, 149; believe owners of Maxwell Grant, 22; census when Agency abandoned at Cimarron, 61; described by Bancroft—Notes, 49; described by Las Vegas Gazette, 63; Kit Carson on, 50; Removal to Maxwell Land Grant, 47; Removed from Maxwell Land Grant, 65; removal to Mescalero Agency at Ft. Stanton, 55; trade with Maxwell, 37; treaty abrogated by U. S. Grant, 64; view of Padre Martinez, 48.
Johnson, President Andrew, appointment of Elkins as United States Attorney, 149.
Johnson, James L., 88.
Johnson Ranch, 120.
Jones, Andrieus A., early life, 142; employment as attorney by Charles Springer, 142; fee from Springer, 143, 144, 145, 146, 147, 148; litigation with Dawson, 142; suit against Springer and Dawson, 144; testimony in Springer fee case, 145; verdict in Springer fee case, 146.
Jones, Calvin, first acquaintance with Lucien B. Maxwell, 90; witness in Maxwell Land Grant suit, 88.
Julian, George W.—Appointment as Surveyor-General, 125; 126-132.
Justice Miller, opinion in Maxwell Land Grant appeal, 110.
Kearney, Brig. Gen. S. W., 25; appointment of Beaubien as Judge, 26.
Keyes, Captain A. S. B., 31, 32, 33—Notes, 33.
Kimberly, Deputy, 104.
King, Ed, 105.
King of Spain—Confirm land grant titles, 4; Supreme Council of the Indies, 3.
Kingdom of Spain—Interest in New Mexico and welfare, 4.
Kiowas, 51; peace with, 53.
Kirkman, Captain Joel, 105.

Kit Carson (See Carson, Christopher).
Koogler, John G.—View on Indian situation, 58.
La Cinta, 73.
La Favre, Manuel, 91.
Lambert, Henry—cook for U. S. Grant, picturesque character, White House, 70.
Lambert, Henry—Johnson Ranch, 120.
Lambert, Henry — owner of St. James Hotel, 69.
Land Distribution under Spanish Law, 5.
Land Grant Boundaries, enlargement of, 10.
Land Grants, confirmation by United States Congress, 11.
Land Grants, political influence, 5.
Land Grants in New Mexico, estimated area, 125.
Land Grant policy of Mexico, inconsistency of, 5.
Land Grant Ring, 129.
Land Grant Titles Complication, Governor Ross on, 10.
Land Grant Titles—Governor L. Bradford Prince, 10.
Land Grant Titles, Mexican Rule, 4.
Land Grant Titles, reasons for granting, 6.
Land Grant Titles, Spanish Rule, 4.
Land Stealing, 125.
Land Titles in New Mexico—by Frank W. Springer, 131.
Land Titles, uncertainty of, 4.
Larrazola, O. A., testimony in Jones-Springer fee case, 146.
Las Animas County, Colorado, 87.
Las Animas Leader, 73.
Las Vegas, 67, 72, 73, 74.
Las Vegas and Vinita Mail and Express Line, 73.
Las Vegas Gazette, 68; October 5, 1872, 58; February 20, 1875, 150; February 28, 1875, 71; July 26, 1875, Lucien B. Maxwell's death, 38; December 25, 1875, 60; September 30, 1876, description of Jicarilla Apaches at Cimarron and Tierra Amarilla, 63; October 7, 1876, 70; March 25, 1880, editorial on Grant Company, 116; April 12, 1884, 74; May 28, 1884, editorial on work of O. P. McMains, 85; February 12, 1876, 72; April 6, 1878, 77; April 26, 1884, Dorsey Ranch, 139.
Laughlin, Pomeron, negro, 69.
Lavat, Paulita Jaquez, 25.
Law of Nations, 126.

Leahy, Jeremiah, testimony in Jones-Springer fee case, 146.
Lee, Bob, 104.
Lee, Jesse, 105, 106; quarrel with John Dodds, 103; shot John Curry, 104.
Lee, Judge William D., attorney for Rev. O. P. McMains, 77.
Lee, Willis T.—Notes, 34.
Lelton, R. P.—Raton Vigilantes, 102.
LeRoux, Joaquin, 94.
Lincoln County War, 67.
Little Buttercup Saloon, 85.
Littrell, Marion, 105.
Littrell, Sam — anti-grant trouble, 103.
Livestock industry, 21.
Loewenstein, Benjamin, 77.
Long, Judge, 139; Farewell to Whitney County Bar, 138.
Longwill, R. H., 55, 96.
Lopez, Julian, 120.
Losch, Acting Governor, 105.
Low, William, witness in Cruz Vega murder case, 78.
Lucero, Pablo, 17.
Lucero, Rafael, 120.
Lynch, Matt—purchase of Maxwell ditch, 37.
Lynches—ejectment suit against, 119.
Maes, Nestor, 77.
Mail Route, Las Vegas to Vinita, 74.
Mail Service, Trinidad to Santa Fe, 150.
Maize, Robert W., 145.
Manco de Burro Pass, 90.
Manila—George Curry, Chief of Police, 101.
Marmon, Robert G., 87, 88, 94.
Marshall, Thomas R., 138.
Martin, Thomas, 84.
Martinez, Antonio, 120.
Martinez, Antonio Jose, Rev., 15, 16, 17; letter regarding Indian situation in New Mexico, 47; letter to J. R. Doolittle, 48; prophecy come true, 120; Note, 123.
Martinez, Felipe Rivera y, 146.
Martinez, Narciso, 120.
Masterson, "Bat," 99.
Masterson, James H. (Jim), arrest by George Curry, gun on J. E. Herndon, 100; escort to Colorado line, 102.
Maury, William A., 109.
Maxwell, Deluvina, capture by Indians, member of Maxwell family, Billy the Kid, 35.
Maxwell, Hugh Charles H., 25.
Maxwell Land Grant, 11, 21; accused of importing Jim Masterson, accused

of misleading Governor Sheldon, 100; acreage, 21, 36, 115, 127; acreage confirmed, 111; acreage represented, 113; appeal to Supreme Court by Government, 97; attorneys for, 109; boundaries, 29; brief of J. A. Bentley, 118; claims of ownership, 29; confirmed by Congress of United States, 19; conflict with Charles Bent, 15; decision of District Court of United States, 97; decision of Surveyor-General Pelham, 19; description, 20; difficulties, 83; dimensions, 24; discovery of steam coal, 142; Dorsey on, 130; factions, 24; failure of Government to buy from Lucien B. Maxwell, 65; final decision on appeal, 109; foreclosure of mortgages, 114; gold, 35, 67; Grant rights superior to Indians, Mexicans and Spanish-American settlers, 21; Indians, 30; Indians believe they own it, actual ownership, 23; lease of lands for Utes and Jicarillas, 46; litigation, 82; litigation in Colorado and New Mexico, 87; litigation involving claims of settlers, 119; litigation over Bent fractional interest, 39; litigation, petition for rehearing, 111; mortgages, 113, 114; opinions on title, 114; original petition for, 13; ownership by Lucien B., 27; owners bring pressure for removal of Utes and Jicarilla Apaches to Reservations, patent issued, 44; Plains Indians, 45; railroad to, 150; ratification of Bayne special master's report, 121; recommended for purchase by U. S. for Indians by Carleton, 53; by Kit Carson, 54; resources within boundaries, 29; rights suspended, 17; sale by Lucien B. Maxwell, 33; sale to English capital, 113; setting up monument, 95; settlers, 23; situate in Colfax County since January 25, 1869, 21; sold to Sherwin, 116; suit by Elkins, et al., 87; superior title, 123; Surveyor John T. Elkins, 149; surveys, 29; thought of purchase for Indians, 53; title confirmed in Miranda and Beaubien, 110; title—confirmed by Act of Congress, 115; title to, perfect, 115; types of men attracted, 75; United States' interest, 86; wild animals, 22.

Maxwell, Luz Beaubien, 25, 26, 113.
Maxwell, Marie Odile Menard, 25.
Maxwell, Odile, 30.
Maxwell, Paulita, 30.
Maxwell, Peter Menard, 30; Notes, 36, 37.
Maxwell, Sofia, 30.
Maxwell, Virginia, 30; marriage to Captain A. S. B. Keyes, 31.

Maxwell Land Grant & Railway Company, 83, 95, 96, 113; colonization by, 83; collapse, 116; financed through British pounds and Dutch gilders, 83; financing by Stephen B. Elkins, 149; on appeal to U. S. Supreme Court, 118; period of reorganization, 118; Sherwin on wreck of, 117; stock and bond selling scheme, 114; stock grant with foreign breeds of horses, cattle and sheep, 83; successor to, 116; title, 84.

Maxwell Land Grant Company, 116; adverse decision by Federal Court for District of Colorado, 109; anti-grant troubles, 83; charter from King of Netherlands, 119; comments of Julian on, 127; conspiracy alleged, 87; counsel in ejectment case vs. Dawson, 145; Dawson litigation, opinion by Mr. Justice Brown, 143; decrees of court enforced by militia, 100; defense in injunction suit, 121; ejectment suit against John B. Dawson, 142; ejectment suits against settlers, 119; eviction by, 83; granting of original petition by Governor Armijo, 20; injunction suits, 119; litigation, final decision by U. S. Supreme Court, 111; litigation—opinion by Justice Miller, 110; petition, original, 20; policy of dealing with settlers, 119; resistance by Padre Martinez, 15; squatters, 83.

Maxwell, Lucien B., 21, 30, 50, 83, 88, 149; acquired all outstanding interests in the Grant, 42; acquires Bent interest in Grant, 40; acquisition of interests, 27; ancestry of, 25; associate of St. Vrain, 27; Bent, 27; arrival in Taos, 25; assert ownership of Grant, 34; building of Cimarron, 29; business man, 39; consideration—$1,350,000, 113; cook in Fremont's party, 33; cost of Maxwell Grant to him, 43; compromise with Charles Bent heirs, 36; death of, 25, 37; deed to John B. Dawson, 141; deed to Uncle Dick Wootton, 95; erection of buildings at Rayado, 29; estate, 37; failure of Government to purchase for Indians, 65; family, 30; First National Bank of Santa Fe, 36; Fort Sumner property, 36; Fremont expeditions, 27; friend of Indians, 30; grant for rehabilitation of Indians, 65; grave, 26, 38; grist mill, 29, 32; hospitality, 67; hunter, 28; in Taos, 28; Kit Carson, 27; knowledge of gold on Grant, 34; lease of lands for Utes and Jicarilla Apaches, 46; little record of life, 26; litigation with Guadalupe Bent Thompson, 40; loss of Bent interests to Maxwell, 40; management of Grant, 27;

marriage, 25, 39; marriage of daughter Virginia, 32; option to sell Grant, 113; ownership of Grant, 27; patent issued after death, 44; Penitentes, 31; politics, 26; purchase of Guadalupe Miranda interest, 41; ranch, 1848-1868, 30; real estate, 39; Richard Owen, 27; sale of ditch to Matt Lynch, 37; sale of Grant, 35, 113; sale of interest in First National Bank of Santa Fe, 36; settled on the Rayado, 29; trapper, 27; Uncle Dick Wootton, 94; with Christopher Carson, 28; with Fremont, 27.

McAuliffe & Ferguson's Hall, anti-Grant meeting, 85.

McCleave, Captain—policy with Utes and Jicarilla Apaches, 59.

McGaughey, Rev. J., 106.

McMains, O. P., 76, 77, 78, 81, 82, 84, 85, 99; active in anti-Grant cause, 76; affiliation with anti-Grant men, 81; anti-Grant meetings, 85; arrest for murder of Cruz Vega, 77; complaint against Judge Vincent, 137; ejected from ranch on Maxwell Grant, 81; publisher of The Comet, 84; Raton Vigilantes, 102; verdict, 77.

Menard family, 25.

Mescaleros, 46.

Mexican Colonization Act of August 18, 1824—Notes, 11.

Mexican Congress, Article 12 of Decree re land grants, 110.

Mexican Government, contracts for land grants, 5.

Mexican independence established, 5.

Mexico, 3; royal audience, 3.

Mexico City—taken over by Iturbide, 5.

Miles, General Nelson A., Cimarron in 1875, remedies plight of Utes and Jicarillas, 59.

Militia organized in Raton, 99.

Military forces in 1875 under command of Department of Missouri, 71.

Miller, Mr. Justice, opinion in Maxwell Land Grant appeal, 109; opinion on petition for rehearing, 111.

Mills, District Attorney Melvin W., 105.

Mills, Judge (Justice) William J., 145, 146.

Miller, Maulding and Curtis, conveyance of rights in Dawson Mine to Dawson, 142.

Miranda, 22.

Miranda-Beaubien Grant, 11; boundary, 94; Lucien B. Maxwell, 26.

Miranda, Don Pablo, 41, 42.

Miranda, Guadalupe, 13, 30—Notes, 40, 115; execution of quitclaim deed to Lucien B. Maxwell, 42; failed to realize extent or value of Maxwell Land Grant, 40; letter to Charles Beaubien, 40, 41.

Miranda, Pedro, 94.

Misc. Doc. No. 201, 49th Congress, 1st Session, House R. No. 1824, 52d Congress, 1st Session, 119.

Mora, 67; trial of O. P. McMains, 77.

Mora County—Dawson Mine, 141; in Grant, 6.

Moreno Valley, 23; gold discovered, 34.

Morley, W. R., 96; Cimarron News and Elizabeth City Railway Press and Telegraph, 68.

Morris, Charles—negro, 69.

Morris, Pedro, 77.

Moulton Hotel, 102.

Muache Utes (See Utes), 45; removal to Tierra Amarilla, 55.

Muller, Fred, 42.

National Guards organized in Raton, 99.

Navajos—United States Army resolve to exterminate, 50.

Netherlands, King of, 119.

New Mexico, 85, 86, 128; acquired by United States, 4; Delegate in Congress Elkins, 149; efforts of S. B. Elkins for Statehood, 150; estimated area of land grants, 125; Governor appointed by Viceroy of New Spain, 4; land grants from Spain or Mexico, 3; made a territory under Mexican rule, 5; made a Department of Mexico, 5; northern and central—in Grant, 6; under jurisdiction of Audience of Mexico City, 4; under Kingdom of Spain, 4.

New Mexico colonization, by land grants from Spain or Mexico, 3.

New Mexico Legislature — creates Maxwell Land Grant & Railway Company, 113; McMains, 81; Memorial regarding condition of Indians, 55.

New Mexico Union, October 1, 1872, 57.

Newton—ejectment suit against, 119.

Noble, John W.—Secretary of Interior, 82.

North American Review, 129.

North American Review, Vol. 145, July to December, 1887 pp. 17-31—Notes, 127.

Norton, A. B., Report on Plight of Utes and Apaches, 53.

O'Brien, Judge James—Decree in injunction suit, 122.

Ocate, 22, 67.

Oklahoma, 21.
Old Malaria, 125.
Olympic Dance Hall, 80.
Ortega, Juan, 77.
Ortiz, Blaz, 146.
Ortiz, Gomecindo, 146.
Osfield, J., Jr.—letter re Rev. McMains, 99; Raton Vigilantes, 102.
Otero, 81.
Overland Mail & Express, 71.
Owens, Richard, 19.

Padilla, Iresano, 120.
Padilla, Petrolino, 120.
Padilla, Santos, 120.
Parks, Judge Samuel—dismissal of McMains, 77.
Pecos River—purchase of lands by Maxwell, 36.
Pelham, William — Surveyor-General, 18.
Penitentes—Lucien B. Maxwell, 31.
Perea, Francisco, 120.
Peru, 3.
Philip the Third, 4.
Philippine Islands—Curry Captain, 101.
Piracy of Public Domain, 128, 132.
Plains Indians, 45; expedition against by Kit Carson, 52; trade at Cimarron, 22.
Poe, John W., 35.
Political influence affecting land grant titles, 6.
Politics, 129.
Ponil River, 21, 76.
Pope, Nathaniel, Superintendent of Indian Affairs, report of discontinuance of Cimarron and discontent of Indians, 54.
Porter, H. M., 96.
Preemption Settlement, rights of settlers based on, 119.
Prichard, George W., 136.
Prince, Governor L. Bradford, report on Land Grant Titles, 10.
Private Land Claims Court, 125.
Proclamation, August 1, 1876—Opening Indian land for settlement by citizens of United States; reason for opening up land, 64.
Promoters—land grants to, 5.
Property rights under Treaty of Guadalupe-Hidalgo, 6.
Public Land: Maxwell Land Grant, 119; portion of New Mexico north of San Juan River and east of the Navajo Reservation, 63.
Pueblo Indians, 46.
Pullman, George M., 116, 117.

Quantrell's Band of Guerillas: Capture of Stephen Benton Elkins, 149.
Railway Press and Telegraph, 68.
Rallado (Rayado), 43.
Raton, 90, 125; anti-Grant growth, 84; Masterson, 99, 100; meeting of Vigilantes, 102; militia, 99; saloons, 102.
Raton Comet, 99.
Raton Comet, February 27, 1885.
Raton Mountain, 89.
Raton Rink—meeting of Raton Vigilantes, 102.
Rawhide, 92.
Rayado, 18, 21, 29, 67.
Rayado (Rallado), 43.
Rayado River, 120.
Raymond, Numa, 72.
Red River, 21, (gold), 67.
Report, Com. Private Lands, 52d Congress, 1st Session, No. 1824 accompanying Mis. Doc. 305—July 9, 1892—Notes, 82.
Report of Commissioner of Indian Affairs, 1872—Notes, 55.
Report of J. C. Fremont to Col. J. J. Abert—Notes, 27.
Report of Secretary of Interior 1895-1896, p. 498—Notes, 22.
Report of the Acting Commissioner of Indian Affairs, 1867—Notes, 53.
Report of the Condition of Indian Tribes published in 1867 by Government Printing Office, pp 358 and 486 —Notes, 49.
Republican party: in power, 152; Catron, leader in, 152.
Rico, 89.
Rinehardt, Isaiah, 31; witness in McMains' murder trial, 77.
Rinehardt, Isaiah, Mrs., 31, 32.
Rinehart, Sheriff I., 70.
Rio Arriba—in Grant, 6.
Rio Arriba County, Catron, in, 152.
Rio Arriba County War, 67.
Rio de la Plata (Buenos Aires), 3.
Rio Grande—land along favored for grants, 6.
Ritch, W. G., 71.
Rito Plain, 22.
Rocky Mountain Herald, 72.
Rogers, Dick, 104; funeral services, 106; Raton Vigilantes, 102.
Romero, Jesus Maria, 146.
Romero, Juan, 120.
Ross, Governor Edmund G., 9, 10.
Royal Audience, 3.
Saavedra, Noverto, 77.
Salazar, Juan Jose, 146.
Saloons—Raton, 102.

Sanchez, Pedro, 120.
San Diego (St. James) Hotel, 70.
Sandoval, Domingo, 120.
Sandoval, Juan, 120.
Sandoval, Romulo, 120.
Sandoval County—in Grant, 6.
San Francisco Mesa, 89, 90.
San Hilario, 73.
San Juan River, 150.
San Miguel—in Grant, 6.
Santa Ana, General Don Antonio Lopez, letter from Antonio Jose Martinez, 47.
Santa Fe, 72; in Grant, 6.
Santa Fe New Mexican—December 8, 1878.
Sarlangre, A. A. De, 117.
Scheurich, Aloys, 43.
Scheurich, Teresina Bent, 43.
Schools, in 1785, 71.
Scroggins, George W., 77.
Secretary of Interior, 128.
Segura, Clemente, 146.
Settlers, believe themselves owners of Grant, disappointment at Supreme Court decision, 112; plight of, 122.
Sheldon, Governor Lionel A.—National Guards, 99.
Sherman, Frank R.—promotion of Grant Company, 116; reorganizes Maxwell Company, 117; testimony on boundaries of Maxwell Grant, 117.
Shout, Dr. J. H., 37.
Showalter, I. C.—Raton Vigilantes, 102.
Sierra Grande, 93.
Silva, Jesus, 36, 94.
Sinnock, Rev. J. W., 106.
Small Holding Claims—Notes, 11.
Small, Justice of Peace—Springer, 103.
Smith, James, 105.
Solano, Ana Maria, 120.
Solis, Julian, 77.
South, Will, 106.
Spanish-Americans, ejectment suits by Maxwell Land Grant Company, 120.
Spanish-American Settlers, plight of, 122.
Spanish Law—appoint governors—for pacification of New Mexico; grant lands, 4.
Spanish-Mexican settlers, citizens under terms of treaty—Guadalupe Hidalgo, 122.
Spiess, Charles A., 145.
Springer, anti-Grant trouble, 103; riot, 125; testimony in litigation taken at, 121; threats at, 100.
Springer, Charles, 142; check to A. A. Jones, 147; interest in Dawson Ranch—Mine, 145; testimony in Jones fee case, 146.
Springer, Frank W., 87, 136, 142; affidavit for temporary injunction, 121; attack on Surveyor-General Julian, 131; attorney for Maxwell Land Grant, 109; attorney for Rev. O. P. McMains, 77; Cimarron News and Elizabeth City Railway Press and Telegraph, 68; defense in Maxwell litigation, 96; director of Maxwell Company, 145; eulogy for Rev. Tolby, 76; Maxwell Land Grant litigation, 121; on Land Titles in New Mexico, 131; suit against settlers, 120; victory in Supreme Court, 111, 112.
Squatters' Club, 84.
Squatters' rights, 23.
St. James Hotel, 69.
St. Vrain, Colonel, 92; associate of Lucien B. Maxwell, 27.
Stage line, 72.
Star Route—Notes, 140.
Star Route mail, fraud charges, 128, 135—Notes, 140.
Stevens, D. W.—employer of George Curry, 100; Raton Vigilantes, 102.
Stockton, Ike, 67.
Stockton, Port, 67.
Sugar Beets, 14.
Supreme Council of the Indies, 3.
Supreme Court of United States, 23, 84, 86, 87, 128; appeal by Government from Judge Brewer's decision, 97; arguments in Grant appeal, 109; confirmed title to Grant in Miranda and Beaubien, 110; final decision in Grant case, 111.
Surveyor-General of New Mexico—creation of office, 126.
Surveyor-General of New Mexico Julian, 125, 126, 127, 128, 129, 130, 131, 132.
Sweetwater, 22.
Taft, William Howard—Philippines, 101.
Taos, 46, 67, 73, 93, 121.
Taos County, 77; record of power of attorney from Miranda to his son Don Pablo, 42.
Taos County District Court, Charles Bent—Maxwell litigation, 39.
Taos, Curate of, 15.
Tascosa, 73.
Taylor, N. G., 53.
Teats, J. H.—owner of Las Vegas and Vinita Mail and Express Line, 73.
Territory of New Mexico, expenditure for subduing Indians, 47.
Texans—Comanche Indian controversies, 57.

Texas, 24.
Texas Panhandle, 73.
The Comet, 84.
The Railway Press and Telegraph, 68.
The Regimental Flag, 72.
Thomas, B. M., Report—August 20, 1877, to Commissioner of Indian Affairs, 62.
Thompson, George W., 39.
Thompson, Jacob, 131.
Tierra Amarilla, removal of Muache Utes to, 55.
Titles to New Mexico Lands, uncertainty of, 4.
Tolby, Rev. T. J., murder of, 75; rehabilitate Utes and Apaches, 76; reward offered by Governor Axtell, 76.
Trading, Indian custom to cease wars during, 22.
Trans-Missouri empire, 72.
Travels in the Great Western Prairies, Thomas J. Farnham, 1843—Notes, 27.
Treaty of Guadalupe Hidalgo, 122, 126.
Trinchera, 95.
Truhillo, 89.
Trujillo, Concepcion, 77.
Trujillo, Rumaldo, 146.
Trujillo, Vidal, conveys to Lucien B. Maxwell, 43.
Twitchell, R. E., testimony in Jones-Springer fee case, 146.
Una de Gato, 21, 89, 128.
Union Spy, accusation against Stephen B. Elkins, 149.
United States—Involved in affairs of Grant, 86.
United States Army, war of extermination against Apaches and Navajos, 50.
United States District Court in Colorado, 87.
United States District Court—for District of Colorado—Adverse Decision in Maxwell Land Grant case, 109.
United States of America—confirmed claim of Maxwell Land Grant, 115.
United States Government, thought of purchase of Maxwell Land Grant for Indians, 53.
United States Indian Agent, lease with Maxwell for Utes and Jicarillas, 46.
United States-Mexico line, 93.
United States vs. Maxwell Land Grant Co., 26 Fed., 118, 97.
United States vs. The Maxwell Land Grant Company et al, 121 U. S. 325, 30 L. Ed. 949—Notes, 109.
United States v. The Maxwell Land Grant Company et al, 122 U. S. 365, 30 L. Ed. 1211—Notes, 111.
U. S. 10th Infantry, 105.
Urioste, David, 146.
Utahs (See Utes)
Ute Indians (See Utes)
Utes, 76, 93, 107, 122; believe owners of Maxwell Grant, 22; census at Cimarron when abandoned, 60; described by Bancroft—Notes, 49; fall of 1875—General Nelson A. Miles—orders resumption of rations, 59; headquarters near Maxwell Ranch, 30; Kit Carson on, 50; removal to Maxwell Land Grant, 47; removed to Colorado, 60; removed from Maxwell Land Grant, 65; report on plight by A. B. Norton, 53; trade with Maxwell, 37; view of Padre Martinez, 48; whiskey trade, 46; willingnesss to attack Kiowas, 51.
Ute Creek—gold, 34.
Valdez, Jose Maria, 94.
Valdez, Juan, 120.
Vandever, William, personal inspection of Indians at Cimarron, report to Commissioner of Indian Affairs November 15, 1877, 62; recommendations regarding removal of Indians, 63.
Van Hall, F. A., 117.
Van Limburg-Stirum—Count, 117.
Veeder, John D., testimony in Jones-Springer fee case, 146.
Vega, Cruz, lynching of, 79; suspected of killing Rev. Tolby; murder of, 76.
Venezuela, 3.
Vermejo, 21, 69, 102.
Vialpando, Francisco, 120.
Vice Royalties, 3.
Viceroy in Mexico City, 4.
Vigil, Bartolo, 120.
Vigil, Cornelio, 15, 94.
Vigilantes, 78; Colfax County, 99; disband, 107.
Vincent, Chief Justice William A., complaint by Rev. O. P. McMains, 137; suspension by President Cleveland, 135.
Vinita, Indian Territoy, 74.
Waddingham, Wilson, 113.
Waldo, Henry L., verdict in O. P. McMains' murder case, 77.
Walker, Hon. Francis A., 54.
Wallace, Francisco, 146.
Wallace, Lew—Notes, 10.
Washington, inability to understand geography of New Mexico and situation of Indians, 63.

Watrous, 105.
Watts, John S.—Notes, 36.
Webb, W. R., 136.
West Virginia, 151, 152.
Whealington, Tom (Red River), 104.
Wheeler, George M.—G. S. Annual Report—Notes, 34.
Whigham, Harry, 87, 118; testifies at Grant trial, 95.
Whiskey, 46.
White, James, 91.
Whitefords—ejectment suit against, 119.
Williams, Bill, 28, 94.
Williams, Jack, 104.
Williamson, Hon. J. A., alleged conspiracy, 82.

Willow Creek—gold, 34.
Wittford, Edward, 84.
Wootton, Richens Lacy (Uncle Dick), 91, 92, 95.
Wootton, Uncle Dick, witness at Grant trial in Colorado, 94.
Younger, Cole, rescue of Stephen B. Elkins, 149.
Younger, Jim, rescue of Stephen B. Elkins, 149.
Yucatan, 3.
Yutas (Utes) 49.
Zamora, Emerjildo, 120.
Zamora, Jose, 120.
Zamora, Librado, 120.
Zamora, Pablo, defendant in Grant litigation, 120.
Zamora, Vicente, 120.
Zielgelaar, F. H., 117.